War Beyo:
Dragon Pagoda

THE KEE-WONGEE

War Beyond the Dragon Pagoda

A Personal Narrative of the
First Anglo-Burmese War
1824 – 1826

Major J. J. Snodgrass

LEONAUR

War Beyond the Dragon Pagoda: A Personal Narrative of the
First Anglo-Burmese War 1824 - 1826
by J. J. Snodgrass

Originally published in 1827 under the title:
Narrative of the Burmese War, Detailing the Operations of
Major-General Sir Archibald Campbell's Army, from its
Landing at Rangoon in May, 1824, to the Conclusion
of a Treaty of Peace at Yandaboo, February 1826

Published by Leonaur Ltd

ISBN: 978-1-84677-233-7 (hardcover)
ISBN: 978-1-84677-234-4 (softcover)

http://www.leonaur.com

Publisher's Notes

In the interests of authenticity, the spellings, grammar and place names
used have been retained from the original edition.

The opinions expressed in this book are those of the author
and are not necessarily those of the publisher.

Contents

Preface

The misstatements and misrepresentations which had at different times appeared relative to the situation and operations of the army lately serving in Ava, under Major-General Sir Archibald Campbell, induced me, during a tedious voyage from Bengal, to draw up the following Narrative. I had, indeed, collected some materials for entering more fully into an account of the interesting and still imperfectly known countries the army traversed on its route to Ava; but conscious that the hurried notes of a soldier, taken while employed on active service in the field, could not afford sufficient data for such an undertaking I have abandoned that intention and, in its present mutilated, though strictly military form, I now present my Journal to the public, without pretension of any kind beyond that of accuracy in the details it may contain. I have only farther to premise, that I left the army at Melloone, with the treaty of peace, concluded at that place, and did not return in time to witness the closing scene of the eventful contest.

J. J. Snodgrass

CHAPTER 1

The Invasion of Burma

The unprovoked aggressions of the Burmese governors of Arracan upon the south-east frontier of Bengal, and the contemptuous silence of the court of Ava to every remonstrance upon the subject, in the beginning of 1824, compelled the Indian government to resort to other measures for obtaining redress, and preventing the future encroachments of a warlike and ambitious neighbour, whose arrogant pretensions and restless character had so frequently interrupted the relations of peace subsisting between the two countries, keeping the frontier provinces in constant dread and danger of invasion. Early in that year orders were given for the equipment of a force of from five to six thousand men at the presidencies of Fort William and Fort St. George: the two divisions were directed to assemble at Port Cornwallis, in the Great Andaman island, from which the combined forces, under the command of Major-General Sir Archibald Campbell, were to proceed for the capture of Rangoon, the principal sea-port of the Burmhan empire.

Between the 12th and 17th of April, the Bengal division, consisting of His Majesty's thirteenth and thirty-eighth regiments and two companies of artillery, were embarked at Calcutta, and the transports immediately proceeded to the place of general rendezvous, which they reached about the end of the month, where a detention of some days took place in consequence of the troops from Madras not having arrived.

During our stay in this romantic bay, frequent excursions were made by parties of officers to different parts of the island, but all their effort to communicate with the few wretched beings who inhabit these sequestered regions were unattended with success; savages, in the fullest sense of the word, they shun the approach of civilised man; and if at any time they are accidentally discovered in the thick-set jungle, which reaches the very edges of the sea, never fail to evince the hostile feelings with which they regard a stranger's visit to their shores, by shooting flights of arrows at the boats, and flying to the interior as soon as a landing is effected.

The Andamaners are very short in stature, and their features bear some resemblance to the inhabitants of the opposite coast of Pegu; their dwellings are huts of the most miserable description, and they appear to be in constant motion in quest of shell-fish, upon which they principally subsist, and in which the bays and creeks of the islands abound. The number of these miserable islanders is very limited, but the impenetrable nature of the woody region they inhabit has hitherto prevented any correct opinion being formed of their habits and condition, every endeavour to hold the slightest intercourse with them, or to ameliorate their wretched situation, having invariably failed. They have been accused of some of the worst propensities of savage man, and have long been considered as cannibals, but probably without sufficient reason; at least the skulls and bones, with which we found their huts plentifully adorned, afforded no ground for such an accusation, which their appearance has sometimes given rise to; but were clearly recognised to have belonged to a species of small island hog, which is frequently caught and used as food by the natives. The origin of these people still remains a subject of conjecture, some supposing, from their woolly hair, that they are of African descent; while others, with equal reason, judging from their countenances, believe them to have come originally from the opposite coast of Pegu, or Arracan.

On the 4th of May, the greater part of the troops from

Madras, consisting of His Majesty's forty-first regiment, a company's European regiment, and several battalions of native infantry, having arrived at Port Cornwallis, orders were given for the sailing of the fleet on the following morning; a small force being at the same time detached under Brigadier M'Creagh, for the capture of the island of Cheduba, and another detachment proceeding under Major Wahab, of the Madras army, for the reduction of the island of Nigrais. On the morning of the 5th, at a signal from His Majesty's ship *Liffy*, Commodore Grant, the fleet accordingly weighed, and put to sea, and on the 10th instant anchored within the bar of the Rangoon river.

The arrival of a British fleet at Rangoon seems to have been wholly unexpected by the Court of Ava; the town was unprepared for its reception, and the civil and military authorities thrown into alarm and consternation. Our arrival was, however, announced by numerous beacons, quickly prepared at the different custom-houses at the mouth of the river, and in the course of the night repeated, by blazing fires, in every part of the surrounding country: it was, therefore, most desirable that no time should be lost in appearing before the town, which we sanguinely hoped would, by accepting our protection, at once place at our disposal the resources of the country in cattle, boats, drivers, and boatmen, with which we were wholly unprovided. In boats especially, Rangoon was known to be well supplied; and it was by many anticipated, that should the king of Ava, upon the capture of his chief commercial city, still refuse to make atonement for his wanton and unprovoked aggressions, that city would afford the means of pushing up the river a force sufficient to subdue the capital, and bring the war at once to a conclusion.

Every necessary arrangement having expeditiously been made, the fleet, next morning, with a fair wind, and led by His Majesty's ship *Liffy*, sailed up the river. A few harmless shots from the Chokies, or guard-houses on its banks, were the only impediments offered to our progress to the town, although, from the intricate navigation and narrow channels through which we had to steer, every ship successively passed within a few feet of a thickly-wooded shore, where a few expert marksmen might with perfect safety have committed the greatest havoc upon our crowded decks.

At twelve o'clock the *Liffy* anchored close to the principal battery at the king's wharf in Rangoon, the transports anchoring in succession in her rear. Having furled sails and beat to quarters, a pause of some minutes ensued, during which not a shot was fired; on our side humanity forbade that we should be the first aggressors upon an almost defenceless town, containing, as we supposed, a large population of unarmed and inoffensive people; besides, the proclamations and assurances of protection which had been sent on shore the preceding day, led us to hope that an offer of capitulation would still be made.

The Burmese, on their part, stood for some time inactive at their guns, apparently unwilling to begin the unequal contest; until, urged by the threats and orders of their chiefs, they at length opened their feeble battery on the shipping. The frigate's fire soon silenced every gun on shore; the enemy, unable to withstand her powerful broadside, fled in confusion from their works, and the troops being landed, took possession of a deserted town. No sooner had the news of our arrival in the river reached Rangoon, than the governor, aware the place could not be defended, directed the whole of the inhabitants to be assembled, and, under the officers and slaves of government, to be driven in a mass to the inmost recesses of the jungle. This is the invariably adopted system of the Burmhan government: the men in such cases are organised into levies and corps, and the unfortunate women and children strictly guarded, as pledges for the good conduct of their fathers, husbands, and brothers, whose desertion or misconduct in the field is punished by the barbarous sacrifice of their nearest female relatives.

The appearance of a town recently taken by storm is, at all times, painful to every man whose feelings have not been blunted by too frequently witnessing the misery such scenes produce among those who, from age or sex, should be exempt from the horrors and calamities of war; and even in the present instance enough remained to awaken pity and regret at the barbarous policy which had driven so many wretched people from their homes, to experience want and ill-treatment from their cruel chiefs, exposed to the inclemency of the weather during the rainy season of the year; but our own situation was such as could not be viewed without uneasiness, rendering us in some measure callous and indifferent to the sufferings of others.

Deserted, as we found ourselves, by the people of the country, from whom alone we could expect supplies, unprovided with the means of moving either by land or water, and the rainy monsoon just setting in—no prospect remained to us but that of a long residence in the miserable and dirty hovels of Rangoon, trusting to the transports for provisions, with such partial supplies as our foraging parties might procure, from time to time, by distant and fatiguing marches into the interior of the country. In the neighbourhood of Rangoon itself, nothing beyond some paddy, or rice, was found: the careful policy of the Burmese authorities had removed far beyond our reach everything that was likely to be of use to an invading army; and it will appear hereafter with how much vigilance and care they followed up the only system which could have rendered the situation and prospects of the invaders seriously embarrassing, or have afforded to themselves a hope of ultimate success.

Another cause of interest and anxiety also claimed our notice; the few British merchants and American missionaries, who were known to be residing at Rangoon, had disappeared, and their too probable fate excited general commiseration throughout the army. It appeared, from the testimony of the few remaining inhabitants of the place, that, at the instant the alarm of our approach was given, all foreigners were immediately seized, strongly fettered; and confined in the king's godown, or custom-house, from which they were repeatedly marched up to the hall of justice, to be examined and interrogated by the governor and his assistants. Ignorant of the equipment, or intended departure of an expedition from India, they were incapable of giving any information on the subject, which by the governor and his colleagues was ascribed wholly to deceit and treacherous designs. Accused of being not only aware of our approach, but of having concerted measures for an attack upon Rangoon with the Indian government, the unhappy prisoners urged their innocence, representing the improbability of their having remained in the country with the knowledge that war was likely to ensue, and the very town they lived in to be invaded by their countrymen, with so many opportunities of quitting a place, under such circumstances, they could not fail to lose their liberty, if even worse did not befall them. But such reasoning, however convincing it may appear to others, was found to have little weight with the provincial tyrants of the Burmhan empire, whose power, when distant from the seat of government, is absolute and uncontrolled, and who, cruel alike from nature and from habit, are seldom to be restrained in their capricious acts of violence and injustice, except by bribery or interest. From a tribunal composed of such officers, little mercy was expected by men who knew them, and whose property, exciting the avarice of their judges, served but to render their destruction the more certain.

Their death was soon resolved on, and they were accordingly sent back to the custom-house, to undergo the sentence that had been passed upon them. In their prison, the guards who surrounded them took a savage pleasure in parading and sharpening the instruments of execution before their eyes, in strewing the sand, and in making the necessary preparations for the work of death. In this dreadful state of suspense they remained for many hours but what neither pity nor remorse could effect, fear at last produced upon the mind of the governor, who, afraid of retaliation, and perhaps not

14

without hopes that, through the means of his prisoners, he might prevent our landing, delayed from hour to hour to give the final order, until the *Liffy's* opening fire upon the town seemed finally to seal their doom, when the timely intrusion of a thirty-two-pound shot into the custom-house, where the authorities were assembled, suspended their deliberations, and hastily broke up the meeting. The chiefs lost no time in leaving the city, and their prisoners, under a small guard, were marched, strongly fettered, some miles into the country. Part of the troops on landing, being pushed a short distance in advance of Rangoon, the guard which accompanied the prisoners became alarmed for their own safety, and lodged their charge in two houses near the great pagoda, where they were next morning found by our advance patrols.

Chapter 2

Rangoon

We had been so much accustomed to hear Rangoon spoken of as a place of great trade and commercial importance, that we could not fail to feel disappointed at its mean and poor appearance. We had talked of its custom-house, its dock-yards, and its harbour, until our imaginations led us to antici-pate, if not splendour, at least some visible signs of a flourish-ing commercial city; but, however humble our expectations might have been, they must have still fallen short of the mis-erable and desolate picture which the place presented when first occupied by the British troops.

The town, if a vast assemblage of wooden huts may be dignified with that name, is surrounded by a wooden stockade, from sixteen to eighteen feet in height, which effectually shuts out all view of the fine river which runs past it, and gives it a confined and insalubrious appear-ance. There are a few brick houses, chiefly belonging to Europeans, within the stockade, upon which a heavy tax is levied; and they are only permitted to be built by spe-cial authority from the government, which is but seldom granted—indeed, it has ever been the policy of the Court of Ava to prevent, as much as possible, both foreigners and natives from having houses of permanent materials, from an idea that they are capable of being converted into places of defence, in which refractory subjects might withstand the arbitrary, unjust, and often cruel measures of their rule.

The custom-house, the principal building in the place, seemed fast tottering into ruins.

One solitary hull upon the stocks marked the dockyard, and a few coasting-vessels and country canoes were the only craft found in this great commercial mart of India beyond the Ganges. One object alone remained to attract universal admiration: the lofty Shoedagon, or Golden Dragon Pagoda, rising in splendour and magnificence above the town, presenting a striking contrast to the scene below. The houses in Rangoon and Ava, generally, are built of wood, or bamboo; those of the former material usually belong to the officers of government, or the wealthier description of inhabitants: the floors are raised some feet above the ground, which would contribute much to their dryness, healthiness, and comfort, were not the space beneath almost invariably a receptacle for dirt and stagnant water, from which, during the heat of day, pestilential vapours constantly ascend, to the annoyance of everyone except a Burmhan. Herds of meagre swine, the disgusting scavengers of the town, infest the streets by day; and at night they are relieved by packs of hungry dogs, which effectually deprive the stranger of his sleep by their incessant howling, and midnight quarrels. Rangoon contains an Armenian and Portuguese church; a strong proof of liberality of sentiment in the government, and of freedom from intolerance and religious prejudice in the people.

There are two roads from town to the Shoedagon, which on either side are crowded with numerous pagodas, varying in size and richness according to the wealth or zeal of the pious architects. These pagodas are all private property, every Burmhan, who can afford it, building one as an offering to Ghaudma; but, when once erected, little care or attention is afterwards paid to them, it being considered much more meritorious to build a new one, even of inferior size, than to repair the old; and numerous ruined towers and pagodas are, in consequence, found in every corner of the kingdom. The Shoedagon stands at the summit of an abruptly rising eminence, at the bottom of which, and at the distance of about two miles and a half, Rangoon is situated. The conical hill, upon which the pagoda stands is seventy-five feet above the road; the area on its top contains upwards of two acres, and in the centre of this space the pagoda is erected—in shape resembling an inverted trumpet, three hundred and thirty-eight feet in height, and surmounted by a cap made of brass, forty-five feet high; the whole is richly gilded.

For many days after the disembarkation of the troops, a hope was entertained that the inhabitants, confiding in the invitations and promises of protection that were circulated about the country, would return to their homes, and afford some prospect of local supplies during the time we were obviously doomed to remain stationary; but the removal of the people from their houses was only the preliminary to a concerted plan of laying waste the country in our front, in the hope that starvation would speedily force the army to leave their shores—a system long steadily persevered in, with a skill and unrelenting indifference to the sufferings of the poor inhabitants, that too clearly marked to what extremes a Burmese government and its chiefs were capable of proceeding, in defence of their country. Every day's experience only increased our disappointment, and proved how little was known of the character of the nation we had to deal with. The enemy's troops and new-raised levies were gradually collecting in our front from all parts of the kingdom; a cordon was speedily formed around our cantonments, capable, indeed, of being forced at every point, but possessing, in a remarkable degree, all the qualities requisite for harassing and wearing out in fruitless exertions the strength and energies of European or Indian troops.

Hid from our view on every side in the darkness of a deep, and, to regular bodies, impenetrable forest, far beyond which the inhabitants and all the cattle of the Rangoon district had been driven, the Burmese chiefs carried on their operations, and matured their future schemes with vigilance, secrecy, and activity. Neither rumour nor intelligence of what was passing within his posts ever reached us. Beyond the invisible line which circumscribed our position, all was mystery or vague conjecture.

It has already been observed, that the army came unprovided with the necessary equipment for advancing either by land or water; indeed it was anticipated, that the capture of Rangoon alone, or at least with that of the enemy's other maritime possessions, would induce the king of Ava to make overtures for peace, and accede to the moderate demands of the Indian government, or, at all events, that the country would afford sufficient water-transport to enable a considerable corps to proceed up the Irrawaddy towards the capital, when little doubt was entertained of a speedy submission to the terms required; nor were the reasons upon which these expectations of aid and assistance from the natives were founded withed some weight. It was urged, that they were not Burmese, but Peguers, and a conquered people, living under the tyrannical sway of a government with which they had for centuries, and often successfully, waged war; deprived of their court, and governed by despotic and mercenary chiefs, whom they obeyed from fear alone; they were represented as discontented with their present situation, and ever longing for their former independence; and finally, that they would easily be induced to join the invading force, and to aid it, by every means in their power, in humbling the tyrant under whose arbitrary rule they had so long suffered every species of degradation. But in these calculations, the well-consolidated power and judicious policy of the government towards its conquered provinces were overlooked, and the warlike and haughty character of the nation was so imperfectly known that no correct judgment could be formed of our probable reception.

With an overgrown opinion of their own prowess and military genius—fostered by frequent victories over all their neighbours, and numerous unchecked conquests during half a century, was it to be wondered at that they should consider the disembarkation of six or seven thousand men upon their coast as a hopeless business, in a country, too, where every man was by profession a soldier, liable at all times to be called upon for military service at the pleasure, of the sovereign. The expectation of deriving resources or assistance of any kind, from a nation so constituted, and living under such a form of government, could no longer be indulged; indeed, from the day the troops first landed, it was obvious that we had been deceived by erroneous accounts of the character and sentiments of the people, and that hostility from both Burmese and Peguer had to be expected.

Could a hope be entertained, after the decided measures that were adopted at Rangoon, that we would yet find native boats and boatmen to carry us six hundred miles up the Irrawaddy, to assail that capital which no Burmhan ever names but with reverence and awe; to overturn that throne which he from infancy has considered as the pinnacle of human power and to confront in hostile array that Prince whose every order is received with dread in the most distant parts of his dominions?

It is besides well known that the boatmen of the Irrawaddy are more particularly attached to, and dependent on, the crown than any other class of men in Ava*, and they proved their devotion to their king by removing every boat that was likely to be useful to us. Such were the situation and prospects of the army at the commencement of the rainy season, the longest, perhaps, that is experienced in any part of India, and during which no troops could keep the field for twenty-four hours together; kept in constant employment by the nightly

---

*Every town on the river, according to its size, is obliged to furnish a gilt, or common war-boat, and to man and keep it in constant readiness; of these his majesty can muster from two to three hundred; they carry from forty to fifty men each, and are, I think, the most respectable part of his force. As they live chiefly by rapine, and are in a state of constant hostility with the rest of the people, they are audacious and prompt to execute any orders, however cruel or violent. *The journal of Captain Cox.*]

irruption of the enemy into our lines, without the means of transporting a gun to assist in driving them from the numerous stockades they had constructed in the immediate vicinity of our posts, for the purpose of rushing in upon the sleeping soldier during the darkness of the night, and without a hope of inducing the inhabitants to break through the cruel thraldom in which they were held.

To form a correct idea of the difficulties which opposed the progress of the invading army, even had it been provided with land-carriage, and landed at the fine season of the year, it is necessary to make some allusion to the natural obstacles which the country presented, and to the mode of warfare generally practised; by the Burmese. Henzawaddy, or the province of Rangoon, is a delta formed by the mouths of the Irrawaddy, and with the exception of some considerable plains of rice-ground, is covered by a thick and tenacious jungle, intersected by numerous creeks and rivers, from whose wooded banks an enemy may, unseen and unexposed, render their passage difficult and destructive.

Roads, or anything deserving that name, are wholly unknown in the lower provinces. Footpaths, indeed, lead through the woods in every direction, but requiring great toil and labour to render them applicable to military purposes they are impassable during the rains, and are only known and frequented by the Carian tribes, who cultivate the lands, are exempt from military service, and may be considered as the slaves of the soil, living in wretched hamlets by themselves, heavily taxed and oppressed by the Burmese authorities, by whom they are treated as altogether an inferior race of beings from their countrymen of Pegu. Those Carians generally residing in the interior, at a distance from the large rivers, in their intercourse with one another, and in their occasional visits to the provincial towns, travel by the footpaths of the jungle; but, except by these scattered tribes, the trade and communication between the different parts of the lower provinces are almost wholly carried on by water.

The Burmese, in their usual mode of warfare, rarely meet their enemy in the open field. Instructed and trained from their youth in the formation and defence of stockades, in which they display great skill and judgment, their wars have been for many years a series of conquests: every late attempt of the neighbouring nations to check their victorious career had failed, and the Burmese government, at the time of our landing in Rangoon, had subdued and incorporated into their overgrown empire all the petty states by which it was surrounded, and stood confessedly feared and respected even by the Chinese, as, a powerful and warlike nation. When opposed to our small, but disciplined body of men, it may easily be conceived with how much more care and caution the system to which they owed their fame and reputation as soldiers was pursued—constructing their defences in the most difficult and inaccessible recesses of the jungle, from which, by constant predatory inroads and nightly attacks, they vainly imagined they would ultimately drive us from their country.

CHAPTER 3

The First Action

That the court of Ava had been for many months preparing for a rupture with the government of India, the tone and conduct of the governors of Arracan and the provinces lying contiguous to our frontier, and the assemblage of troops in that quarter, afford the strongest evidence; offensive warfare was obviously intended. But the invasion of their own frontiers, more especially of the distant coasts of Pegu and Tenasserim, seems to have been wholly overlooked in their warlike preparations.

During the preceding cold season, while the British troops occupied the southern part of the Chittagong district, considerable bodies of Burmese had crossed the Arracan mountains; and although they at that time did not venture to show themselves in force upon our frontier, reports were industriously circulated by them, that unless our claim upon the island of Shaporee was speedily relinquished, an army of thirty thousand men would invade Bengal.

On the return of the sickly season in March and April, our troops were compelled to withdraw from the lower parts of the district, leaving at Ramoo, a post about sixty miles to the southward of Chittagong, only a small force, consisting of eight weak companies of Sepoys of the line; a provincial battalion, and a levy of five or six hundred armed Mugs*, to

---

*Natives of Arracan whose families had fled from their country at the period of its conquest by the Burmese.

watch the motions of the enemy, who from this period appear to have been secretly employed in making roads through the jungle, and in other preparations for moving forward, as soon as their numbers were completed to such a strength as would enable them to act upon the offensive. Reinforcements were also sent into Assam and Cassay, both which kingdoms the Burmese monarch held by right of conquest, but in the insalubrious jungles and marshes on the frontiers of Arracan and Chittagong, the hostile chiefs evidently meant to commence their aggressive operations. To that point their views appear to have been exclusively directed, leaving the southern and maritime provinces of the kingdom wholly unguarded, as naturally secure from any attack of their enemy; and it was not until the expedition had actually landed in Pegu, that the possibility of such an event obtained belief at the enemy's capital. When it was represented to the king of Ava, by one of the detenues, as a thing likely to occur, his Majesty laughingly replied, "As to Rangoon, I will take such measures as will prevent the English from even disturbing the women of the town in cooking their rice."

As soon, however, as our actual disembarkation was reported to the government, no time was lost in making the most vigorous. preparations for our expulsion. The war tocsin was sounded in every part of the kingdom; and every town and village, within three hundred miles of the seat of war, speedily sent its complement of armed men, under their respective chiefs, in the fullest confidence of driving the audacious and rebel strangers (as we were designated in all official documents), who had invaded their country, back into the ocean from whence they came. Neither the season of the year, nor the want of an adequate supply of muskets from Ava, were deemed sufficient cause for a moment's delay in the execution of such a service. The royal mandate was no sooner received, than the Irrawaddy was covered with fleets of warriors from the towns upon its banks, proceeding with all possible dispatch to the general rendezvous of the grand army of Henzawaddy; the court and the nation vying with each other in arrogant threats, and professions of contempt for the strangers who had descended on their coast, shut up and surrounded, as we were supposed to be, in a distant corner of the empire.

Towards the latter end of May, the enemy became more daring as their troops rapidly increased in numbers; and approaching gradually upon the British position, commenced stockading themselves in the jungle, within hearing of our advanced posts. Their approaches met with every possible encouragement from the British commander, who, unable to undertake any distant operation, was only careful to give full scope to the natural arrogance of his enemy, which he was well aware would lead them to afford him abundant opportunities of making such an impression upon their troops, as he hoped might still induce the court of Ava to sue for peace. Nor were we long kept in expectation of such an opportunity.

On the morning of the 28th of May, the enemy, having stockaded an advanced corps within little more than musket shot distance-from our piquets, Sir Archibald Campbell, with four companies of Europeans from His Majesty's thirteenth and thirty-eighth regiments, two field-pieces, and four hundred native infantry, moved out to reconnoitre; it having been reported, that the stockade immediately in our front was supported by the governor of Shudaung, with a considerable force, stationed for the purpose of carrying on a desultory warfare with our posts, and preventing the inhabitants of Rangoon, who were said to be kept in the jungle in his rear, from returning to their homes.

A few minutes' march brought our advance-guard in contact with the first stockade, erected upon the pathway by which the troops advanced, with its shoulders thrown back into the jungle on either flank. The work being still incomplete, little opposition was made, the Burmese retiring through the wood after discharging a few shots. The column continuing to advance along a winding pathway, scarcely admitting two men to march abreast, at every opening of the jungle parties of the enemy were seen retiring slowly in our front; and at every turn of the road, breastworks and half-finished stockades, hastily abandoned, proved that so early a visit was neither anticipated nor provided for. After an advance of five miles, the road suddenly entering some rice-fields, intersected by a morass and rivulet, rendered passable by a long and narrow wooden bridge, the enemy was here seen in some force, attempting a formation, for the purpose of defending the passage; but the fire of the two field-pieces compelling them to abandon that intention, they continued their retreat into the woods.

The weather, which had hitherto been fine, now threatened one of those storms which generally usher in the southwest monsoon: the rain began to fall in torrents, the guns could be dragged no farther, and the native infantry were in consequence left to guard them; the General having determined to push on rapidly with the four European companies, as far as the plain of Joazoang, in the hope of liberating some of the peaceably-disposed inhabitants from their military despots; well assured that, if successful, their release would be followed by the subsequent desertion of their male relations, for whose fidelity they were held in pledge. The road again entering the jungle, continued winding through it for upwards of a mile, until at length the extensive plain of Joazoang opened in our front. It appeared about four miles in length, and nearly one in breadth; bounded on one flank by a thick, continued jungle, and on the other by a creek, the banks of which were also covered with a belt of brushwood. About a mile distant from where the column emerged from the forest, and situated in a narrow gorge of the plain, flanked by jungle on either hand, and at no great distance apart, stood the villages of Yanghoo and Joazoang: behind these villages appeared a cloud of smoke, as if proceeding from a concourse of people cooking; and we now confidently anticipated the pleasure of breaking through the cordon of annoyance that had so long surrounded us, and of liberating the people of Rangoon from their state of bondage.

The storm still continued with great violence; but with the prospect of employment before them, the soldiers cheerfully marched on, knee deep in water, through the rice-grounds. The enemy was now seen in such considerable bodies, moving out from the rear of the villages, as to leave no doubt that the smoke we had perceived proceeded from their encampment, and not, as we had supposed, from an assemblage of friends. Their generals on horseback appeared busily employed forming their men for the defence of the gorge, or narrow passage in our front; while the four British companies continued to advance, by echelon of companies, upon a force that appeared to consist of not less than from four to five thousand men. Our left flank, which led close in with the jungle, on approaching the villages, observed that they were defended in front by two stockades, from which shouts and cries of "Laghee! laghee!" (Come! come!) soon satisfied us they were filled with men confident in themselves, and in the strength of their position.

They at once commenced a heavy fire upon the leading companies, to which, from the wet state of their muskets, our troops could at first make but little return: not a moment was therefore lost in closing with their opponents; the right company being directed to hold its line on the plain in check, while the other three rushed forward with irresistible impetuosity to the works in front, and as they were of a low description, not exceeding eight feet in height, soon forced their way into the interior, where the very numbers of the enemy creating disorder and confusion, proved their final ruin. The conflict that ensued was fierce and sanguinary. The work having only one or two narrow ways of egress the defendants, driven from the ramparts, soon became an unmanageable mass; and rendered desperate by the discharges of musketry that were now poured in among them, they, with spear or musket couched, and their heads lowered to a butting position, blindly charged upon the soldiers' bayonets; for until they had long subsequently been taught by severe retaliation to treat with mercy those whom the fortune of war might place in their power, the Burmese neither gave nor expected quarter, but continued fighting with the utmost fury long after all hope of success or escape had ceased to encourage them in continuing the conflict, nor did it remain optional with the soldiers to spare the lives of an enemy from whose barbarous and treacherous mode of warfare death alone afforded safety.

The experiment, indeed, was often tried, but tried in vain. Humanity might prompt a British soldier to pass a fallen or vanquished foe, but when he found his forbearance repaid on all occasions by a shot, the instant that his back was turned, self-preservation soon taught him the necessity of other measures; and it consequently happened, that our first encounters with the troops of Ava were sanguinary and revolting, especially, to soldiers whom feeling and the customs of war alike taught to treat with kindness and forbearance those whom their valour had subdued.

During the attack upon the two stockades, the enemy's General on the plain made no movement to assist in their defence, either trusting with confidence to the garrisons he had left in them, or believing we had a much greater force kept purposely out of sight, and masked by the jungle in our rear; but the instant our troops were seen in possession of the works, the whole line, with a horrid yell, began to move towards us, until checked by the company now extended in their front and the appearance of the troops which had carried the stockades also moving rapidly forward, and forming in readiness to receive their new opponents. Our killed and wounded were then carried from the field, when the enemy, not thinking proper to attack, and the day drawing near its close, we commenced our march slowly, and unmolested, back to quarters, leaving four hundred of the enemy dead on the field.

CHAPTER 4

Operations at Kemmendine

Every effort to communicate either to the court of Ava, or to the commanders in our front, the terms upon which the government of India was still ready to conclude a peace, had hitherto failed; and it was not till after the affair of the 28th of May, that a disposition was evinced of listening to a statement of the wrongs which were complained of, and the redress that would be required, before the British forces could leave their shores. Convinced, however, by the specimen they had already received of the military dualities of their enemy, and the consequent expediency of trying to gain time for preparation, the Burmese chiefs at length had recourse to their favourite system of intrigue and cunning, in an attempt to lull their adversaries into inactivity by professions of friendship, while they were busily employed in fortifying their position, and in completing and equipping their army. The value of such professions, from men proverbially false and deceitful, was duly appreciated by the British commander, who was well aware that the main body of the enemy had taken post at Kemmendine, where they were labouring incessantly, day and night, to render their position proof against the utmost efforts of the British force. The village of Kemmendine, situated on the river, only three miles above Rangoon, was a war-boat station and chiefly inhabited by the king's war-boat men. The ground behind the village, elevated and commanding, is surrounded by a thick forest in its rear. The heights had already been strongly stockaded and abatised in front; the approach on the land-faces was also rendered difficult by a thick and extensive jungle, and the swampy nature of the ground towards the river strengthened the work on that side.

Arrangements were already made for attacking this post, when, on the morning of the 9th of June, a request was sent in from the enemy's camp, that two men of rank, desirous of conferring with the English general, might be furnished with passports, and allowed to come into Rangoon by water. Leave was immediately granted and in the course of the forenoon two war-boats made their appearance, from which the deputies landed, and were conducted to the house where the British commissioners were waiting to receive them.

The principal personage of the two, who had formerly been governor of Bassien, was a stout, elderly man, dressed in a long scarlet robe, with a red handkerchief tied round his head, in the usual Burmhan style. His companion, although dressed more plainly, had much more intelligence in his countenance; and notwithstanding his assumed indifference, and humble demeanour, it soon became evident, that to him the management of the interview was entrusted, though his colleague outwardly treated him in every respect as an inferior.

The two chiefs having entered the house, sat down with all the ease and familiarity of old friends; neither constraint nor any symptom of fear appeared about either: they paid their compliments to the British officers, and made their remarks on what they saw with the utmost freedom and good-humour. The elder chief then opened the subject of their mission, with the question, "Why are you come here with ships and soldiers?" accompanied with many professions of the good faith, sincerity, and friendly disposition of the Burmese government. The causes of the war, and the redress that was demanded, were again fully explained to them. The consequences of the line of conduct pursued by their generals, in preventing all communication with the court, was also pointed out, and they were brought to acknowledge, that a free and unreserved discussion of the points at issue could alone avert the evils and calamities with which their country was threatened.

Still they would neither confess that the former remonstrances of the Indian government had reached their king, nor enter into any arrangement for removing the barrier they had placed in the way of negotiation, but urged, with every argument they could think of, that a few days' delay might be granted, to enable them to confer with an officer of high rank, then at some distance up the river: they were, however, given to understand, that delay and procrastination formed no part of our system, and that the war would be vigorously prosecuted, until the king of Ava thought proper to send officers, with full authority to enter upon a treaty with the British commissioners.

The elder chief, who had loudly proclaimed his love of peace, continued chewing his betel-nut with much composure, receiving the intimation of a continuance of hostilities with more of the air and coolness of a soldier who considered war as his trade, than became the pacific character he assumed; while his more shrewd companion vainly endeavoured to conceal his vexation at the unpleasant termination of their mission, and unexpected failure of their arts and protestations. But although the visit had evidently been planned for no other purpose than that of gaining time, the chiefs did not object to carry with them to their camp a declaration of the terms upon which peace would still be restored; and that they might take their departure with a better grace, expressed their intention of repeating their visit in the course of a few days, for the purpose of opening a direct communication between the British general and the Burmese ministers.

The elder chief, again alluding to his being no warrior, hoped that the ships had strict orders not to fire upon him; but while he said so, in stepping into his boat, there was a contemptuous smile upon his own face and the countenances of his men, that had more of defiance than entreaty in it.

The boatmen wore broad Chinese hats, which sheltered their bodies from the weather, and in some measure softened their harsh, bold, and strongly-marked features. They went off with great speed, rising to their short oars, and singing in chorus, "Oh, what a happy king have we!"

Long before daylight next morning, 10th June, the heavy-rolling noise of gulls in motion, the clattering of arms, and the confused hum of troops in march, announced a movement in the British lines, and warned the enemy at Kemmendine, and in their numerous stockades around us, to prepare for their defence.

The road to Kemmendine by which the troops advanced, runs parallel to, and at no great distance from the river; having a narrow plain of rice-grounds on that side, and on the other a thick and impassable forest. About a mile and a half from Rangoon, the road ascends a gently-sloping hill, at which point the head of the column was received with a smart fire from a stockade, the size and strength of which was hid in the jungle, which on three sides covered its approach. The only visible part of the work appearing from twelve to fourteen feet high, protected in front by abatis, railing, and palisadoes driven into the ground diagonally, and defended by a numerous garrison, who bailed our approach with loud and incessant cheering. To attack the place by escalade would evidently have cost the lives of many, and an attempt to breach it was accordingly directed. Two eighteen pounders being brought within a short distance of the stockade, opened with great effect, and in a few minutes a considerable gap was apparent in its outward defences. The troops destined for the assault, consisting of His Majesty's forty-first regiment, and the Company's Madras European corps, now moved forward, while at the same moment a party of the thirteenth and thirty-eighth regiments in the rear, attacking by escalade, in a few minutes the work was wholly in our possession; the enemy leaving two hundred dead upon the ground, afforded the best proof that could be given of the courage with which their post

had been defended. At the rear gate of the fort, the gilt chattah (umbrella), sword, and spear of the Burmese commander
were found, the chattah much shattered by a shower of grape,
and the body of the chief was found a few yards further in the
jungle, He had apparently received his death wound where
the emblems of command were dropped, and had probably
been carried off by his attendants, until their own safety rendered it expedient to leave their burden behind them. The
chief was said to have been recognized as the elder deputy of
the day before, whose pacific tone had so much amused us.

The road being now open, the column again moved forward to the termination of the rice-grounds, where behind
a belt of jungle appeared a shoulder of the great Kemmendine stockade, stretching down towards the river on one side,
and on the other running off in an oblique direction along
the heights formerly mentioned, and so generally covered
by heavy jungle, as to prevent any correct idea from being
formed of its strength and construction. It was intended, by
again reaching the river above the stockade, to have completely invested it, for the purpose of trying the effect of
mortars upon an enemy unaccustomed to those destructive
engines of modern warfare; and in pursuance of this plan the
rear was halted on the plain in communication with the river
below the place, while the head of the column moved up to
the right, advancing with great difficulty through the wood.

It was only after penetrating for a mile and a half that we
became sensible of the great extent of the position, and the
impossibility of preventing escape from more than a single
face of the principal stronghold; but it was still expected that
the natural obstinacy of the enemy would lead them to await
the bombardment that was intended to commence on the
following morning, the day being too near its close to admit
of an immediate attack. It was five in the afternoon before
the troops were in position, at the distance of only one hundred yards from the stockade, still, however, hid from our
view by the trees, which, extending to within a few yards of

the place, rendered a regular advance impracticable, and any attack that might be made subject to all the disadvantages of a desultory movement; and the troops would be compelled, after debouching from the cover, slowly and individually to force their way through abatis and palisadoes, exposed to all the fire of the garrison. One or two slight openings of the jungle enabled us to get a glimpse of the defences, upon which batteries were erected; and during the night the wood in front was cut down, and every preparation made to render our fire effectual.

The enemy on their part were not idle, but kept us on the alert by repeated attacks in the rear of our line, while their sharp-shooters in trees on every side prevented us from feeling, as we otherwise might have done, all the misery of the wet and uncomfortable situation we were placed in: deluged with rain, and unprovided with shelter of any kind, the night was passed in listening to the frequent cheering of the garrison, and In the hope that a few short hours would afford an opportunity of putting their noisy valour to the test.

The day had scarcely dawned when hostilities commenced, and after a short bombardment, columns of attack being formed, moved forward to the assault; but they only arrived in time to witness the last of the rapidly retreating Burmese, who panic-struck with the dreadful effect of our shells in a crowded stockade, and wholly unprepared for such a salute, bad prudently commenced to evacuate the place soon after the batteries first opened.

Some days of quiet followed the operations at Kemmendine: the enemy, strongly impressed with their recent losses and disappointment, kept at a safer distance from our lines, and the troops, for a short time, suffered less annoyance from nightly visits to their posts; but beyond these temporary advantages, no favourable change took place, either in the situation of the force, or in our future prospects. Not an inhabitant returned to his home: nor was a desire of peace evinced in any measure of the court of Ava. On the contrary, hostility, to the last extremity, had evidently been fully resolved upon; the advances, proposals, and remonstrances of the Indian government were alike treated with silent contempt.

Much has been said of the ignorance in which the king of Ava was kept, regarding the causes and progress of the war; that the communications that had passed between the two countries, both previous to and after its commencement, had been carefully kept from his knowledge; and that his ministers and chiefs, in the full confidence of terminating the contest favourably, continued to keep him in ignorance of the disasters and defeats his troops sustained in the neighbourhood of Rangoon, deceiving him with constant assurances of victories, and the speedy expulsion of the invaders from his kingdom. Nothing, however, proved more incorrect than these conjectures; as abundant opportunities afterwards occurred of ascertaining from many sources, that hostilities were not only sanctioned by his majesty, but that his resolution of attacking our south-east frontier had been publicly announced long previous to the invasion of his own territories; and there is every reason to believe that the country at large applauded the resolution, and looked forward with confidence to the honour and riches that awaited them, in a war with their wealthy neighbours.

It is perhaps to be regretted, that our imperfect knowledge of the nation prevented a more correct opinion from being formed of the probable effects of a landing in their country; and still more unfortunate, that the information of those who had visited Ava should have led us to calculate upon aid, assistance, or supplies, from the natives of Pegu. Experience, however, soon satisfied even the most sanguine, of the value to be placed upon the friendly disposition of the Peguers: instead of improving, our situation gradually became worse; and our very successes, in proving to the enemy with what facility their strongest posts were carried, only tended to convince them of the necessity of removing the means of transport we were so much in want of farther from our reach. The plains, for many miles around us, were swept of their herds; the rivers were un-provided with one friendly canoe; the towns and villages were deserted, and every man beyond our posts in arms against us. Promises of reward and offers of protection, supported with frequent examples of our power to afford it, proved equally unavailing in drawing from their allegiance men brought up in terror of their chiefs, and still impressed with extravagant notions of the talents and resources of their rulers.

The chiefs, on their part, fully confident of the ultimate success of their plans, continued to pursue their desolating system with unrelenting rigour, and with a success that effectually put a stop to further expectations of local aid, and pointed to India as the place from which the means of prosecuting the war must necessarily be derived.

Before the end of June, the enemy appeared to have recovered in a great measure from the panic and dismay occasioned by the reverses they had experienced in the early part of the month. Having received large reinforcements, and supplies of warlike stores, Sykia Wongee (third minister of state), who commanded in chief, again advanced, with positive orders from the king to attack and drive the British at once into the sea. On the 30th and 31st unusual bustle and commotion, in the woods in our front, announced the approaching contest. Eight thousand men were computed to have crossed to the Rangoon side of the river, above Kemmendine, in one day; and the jungles around us seemed animated by an unseen multitude of people: clouds of smoke marked the encampments of the different corps of the Burmhan army in the forest; and their noisy preparations for attack formed a striking contrast to the still and quiet aspect of the British line. The arrival of the eighty-ninth British regiment from Madras, and the junction of the detachments which had captured Cheduba and Negrais, added considerably to the force, which had already been much diminished by sickness and death, brought on by hard service during an inclement season, and the usual casualties of war.

CHAPTER 5
Action Around Rangoon

The Great Dagon Pagoda, in itself a fortress, was occupied by a battalion of Europeans, and may be considered as the key of the British position, the rest, of the force occupying the two roads running from it to the town; the numerous religious edifices convents, and pilgrims' houses upon them, affording good shelter to the troops against the inclemency of the season. Two detached posts completed the position: one at the village of' Puzendown, where the Pegu and Rangoon rivers meet, about a mile below the town; the other at, Kemmendine, for the protection of the shipping against the enemy's fire-rafts.

About mid-day on the 1st of July, the enemy appeared in large bodies issuing from the jungle to the right and front of the Great Pagoda, moving towards Rangoon, in a direction nearly parallel to our position, and detaching a column to the left, which took possession of the upper part of the village of Puzendown, and set it on fire. The main body having arrived within half a mile of Rangoon, their columns rapidly changed front, and commenced a spirited attack upon that part of our line which approached nearest to the town. Their masses, covered by a cloud of skirmishers, having penetrated between two of our piquets, formed upon a hill within musket-shot of the position, and commenced firing from jingals, and other heavy arms. But on the salute being returned by two field-pieces served with grape and shrapnel, their advance was quickly checked; and at the same moment the forty-third Madras native infantry, opposed to them, moving forward in the handsomest style, drove their columns from the hill, and compelled them to seek for safety in a rapid retreat.

During the attack upon our right, parties of the enemy felt our piquets along the line to our left, in front of which his columns were concealed by the jungle, apparently only waiting for the signal to attack. That signal, however, was never given: it depended upon the success that might attend the operations of the left wing, which was to attack vigorously, and having carried any part of our position, the whole Burmese line was to have rushed boldly forward to complete the victory. Such was Sykia Wongee's plan of attack, and having failed in the first part of it, he did not think it expedient to persevere further, but directed a general retreat.

The news of his defeat had no sooner· reached Ava, than the unfortunate Wongee was recalled in disgrace, although in the interim a senior officer, Soomba Wongee, (second minister,) had arrived with considerable reinforcements, and assumed the command of the army of Henzawaddy*.

Convinced, from the ill success of his predecessors, that his troops were not in a state to cope with the British in the field, or in regular warfare, the new commander wisely stockaded his army in the most difficult parts of the forest, at a place called Kummeroot, about five miles from the Great Pagoda, intending, under cover of the night, to carry on such a system of desultory warfare, as would harass, and ultimately destroy our worn-out soldiers. He had also fortified a commanding point upon the river above Kemmendine, in communication with his stockaded camp, and not only obstructing the navigation of the river, but affording an excellent situation for the construction of fire-rafts, by the judicious employment of which he contemplated the destruction of our shipping.

---

*The province of Rangoon named by the Burmese Henzawaddy.

These arrangements completed, the confidence they inspired was soon conspicuous, in the daring inroads of numerous parties, which now paid nightly visits to our lines, and determined the British commander, notwithstanding the incessant rains which fell, to endeavour to bring the Wongee to a general action. The necessary orders to that effect were accordingly given out, and on the morning of the 8th, two columns of attack were formed, Sir A. Campbell embarking with one column for the attack of the enemy's position upon the river, while Brigadier-General M'Bean, with the land column, was directed to move upon Kummeroot, and attack the enemy vigorously on that side.

The position above Rangoon was found sufficiently formidable, and the ground remarkably well chosen. About a mile above Kemmendine the river separates into two branches; the point of land where they divide is bold and projecting, and commands a long reach under it. Upon this point the enemy's principal stockade was erected, provided with artillery, and defended by a numerous garrison. On the opposite bank of either branch stockades and other defences were erected, enfilading the approach to the principal work, and all mutually defending each other. It was judged necessary to employ breaching vessels, for the purpose of destroying the outward defences of the works, and at nine o'clock a brig and three Company's cruisers, manned by seamen of His Majesty's and the honourable Company's navy, under the superintendence of Captain Marryat, the senior naval officer, dropped with the tide, took their respective stations, and opened a heavy cannonade on the stockade.

The enemy's guns were for some time well served, but they were ultimately silenced by the superior fire from the shipping; and the preconcerted signal of "breach practicable" being displayed from the mainmast-head of the senior officer's ship (Lieutenant Frazer of the navy), the troops destined for the assault, consisting of details from His Majesty's forty-first and seventeenth Madras native infantry, under Lieutenant-

Colonel Godwin and Major Wahab, pushed across the river in boats, and notwithstanding the stakes and other obstacles they had to encounter on landing, in a very short time surmounted every difficulty, and carried the great stockade with comparatively small loss, the enemy suffering severely in killed, and many being drowned in trying to effect their escape.

The operations of the land column on this day were equally successful. Brigadier-General M'Bean on approaching Kummeroot found himself surrounded by stockades, the extent or strength of which could be only partially observed, and in presence of a force whose numbers, when compared with the little column that advanced upon them, warranted in some measure the Burmese chiefs in treating any attempt upon their works, by such a handful, with ridicule and contempt. Unprovided with guns, the Brigadier-General at once formed his troops for the assault, and storming parties from His Majesty's thirteenth, thirty-eighth, and eighty-ninth regiments, rapidly advanced to escalade.

The principal work in the centre of the enemy's line was composed of three distinct stockades, one within another, in the interior one of which, Soomba Wongee, the Burmese commander-in-chief, had established his headquarters, secure in the imagined strength of his position, and in the valour of his men. He was sitting down to dinner when the approach of the British troops was first announced to him; and merely directing his chiefs to proceed to their posts, and "drive the audacious strangers away," the haughty Wongee, without seeming to pay more attention to the report, was proceeding with his forenoon repast, when the rapid musketry of the assailants at length convinced him that the utmost courage and exertion would be required to save him from defeat, disgrace, and probably from the vengeance of his sovereign: urged by these considerations, Soomba Wongee, contrary to the ordinary custom of Burmese commanders, placed himself at the head of his retreating troops, and encouraged them by his voice and his example, to offer a steady resistance to their advancing foes.

His two first lines, already routed with dreadful slaughter, were crowding into the centre stockade, followed by the British soldiers, whose unremitting and destructive fire upon the confused and penned-up mass rendered all the exertions of their chiefs to restore any degree of order fruitless and unavailing. Wongees and Woondocks, officers and men indiscriminately mixed together, unable to fly, charged the British soldiers with the fury of despair, but their efforts and resistance only tended to augment their losses and complete their final route.

Soomba Wongee, a Woondock, and several other chiefs of rank, with eight hundred men were killed upon the spot, and the jungle and villages in the neighbourhood were filled with the unhappy wretches who were wounded, and left to die, from want of food and care. The disastrous consequences of the action of the 8th failed not to make a deep impression on the enemy and to redouble the caution and prudence of their chiefs. The ease and celerity with which the British troops had in one day captured ten stockades provided with thirty pieces of artillery, and garrisoned by vastly superior numbers, convinced the leaders of the Burmese army, that their strongest fortifications insured no certain protection against such assailants, whose skill and resources afforded on all occasions the means of overcoming obstacles which, in all their former wars, had been deemed insurmountable; and the Burmese troops were no less satisfied that no numerical superiority could place them on a footing with soldiers whose rapid and combined movements, covered by a destructive and sustained fire, rendered their own hurried and irregular efforts only productive of confusion and consequent defeat.

On the 11th instant a party of reconnaissance visited the captured stockades, but saw nothing of the enemy. Several wounded Burmese were found lying about the place, and were brought into our hospitals, but unfortunately none of them recovered. They said the stockade had been visited on the 9th by parties of their countrymen, sent for the purpose of collecting balls, and such muskets or other weapons as might have been left undestroyed. These men gave their wounded comrades a most deplorable account of the army; their loss they represented as immense, stating that the villages, for many leagues behind, were crowded with their wounded; and that desertions to a great extent were daily taking place. They left food and water with the wounded men, but as their wounds were considered mortal, no offer of further aid was made, or desire expressed of being moved: in such cases the unhappy sufferer is generally left to his fate, which he meets with fortitude and resignation; and if at any time pain compels him to solicit aid, it is only that a speedy period may be put to his sufferings.

A considerable time now elapsed without any occurrence beyond a few partial affairs of posts. The rains were at their height, and the adjacent country almost wholly underwater. Sickness, to an alarming extent, had made its appearance among the troops, and the prospect of a successful termination to the contest became daily more gloomy and uncertain. The enemy, on their part, rendered more cautious and circumspect by experience, kept at a safer distance from our front, but continued to add to the sufferings of our troops, by frequent nocturnal visits and successful exertions in preventing our foraging parties from obtaining the supplies which we stood in so much want of. No part, however, of the conduct of their rulers evinced the slightest disposition to come to any explanation on the subject of a peace, the recent misfortunes of their armies only tending to stimulate the court of Ava to more vigorous measures, levying and equipping men for that purpose in every part of the country.

The British commander, disappointed in his expectations of bringing the enemy to terms, by any local operations or successes; and unprovided with the means of carrying the war a day's march into the interior, now resorted, in obedience to his instructions, to attempt the subjugation of his Burmhan majesty's maritime possessions to the eastward, in the hope that their conquest might induce him to listen to reason and accept of terms. For that purpose a small expedition, consisting of His Majesty's eighty-ninth regiment, and the seventh Madras native infantry, under the command of Lieutenant-Colonel Miles, was immediately got in readiness, and, with a considerable naval force, sailed to the eastward. This expedition was attended with complete success; Tavoy surrendered; Mergui was taken by storm, and the whole coast of Tenassarem gladly accepted of British protection; but owing to the unfavourable season of the year, news of these events did not reach Rangoon before the beginning of October, when the war had assumed an aspect that precluded every hope of peace from any event short of the reduction of the capital, or the complete prostration of the power and resources of the nation.

During the latter part of July, finding ourselves in a great measure relieved from the presence of any force in our immediate neighbourhood, the time was considered favourable for attempting the release of such of the inhabitants of Rangoon, as were desirous of returning to their houses, it having been represented that many families of that description were detained by small guards in the villages upon the Puzendown Creek: for that purpose a detachment was embarked on board the steam-vessel and boats of the flotilla, and proceeded up the river; but the vigilance and activity of the Burmese police, even amidst the defeat and disasters of their army, was everywhere conspicuous, in the precautions they had taken to prevent our reaping any advantage from the late occurrences.

At the different villages up the Creek, a great number of large cargo-boats, deeply laden with rice and salt fish, were found in readiness to start for Ava, the moment an opportunity of passing Rangoon occurred; but to us they were rendered useless by their unmanageable construction, the boatmen, who alone can conduct them in safety through the currents and eddies of the river, having fled at the approach of the troops. The whole of this district is very fertile in rice, and a large quantity is annually sent up the Irrawaddy, for the consumption of the capital, and the less fertile provinces of Upper Ava. The large boats above mentioned, in which it is conveyed, make only one trip yearly, being sent down with the first rise of the river, in the beginning of the rainy season; they receive their cargoes, and proceed on their voyage home, when the river is full and during the strength of the south-west monsoon, which enables them to stem the current.

In every village there appeared a small party of military police, who, upon the appearance of the steam vessel and other boats, rigidly enforced the orders of their post, by driving the inhabitants, men, women, and children, from their houses to the jungle, there to remain exposed to the incessant rains, until their guards thought proper to permit them to return. At most of the villages we found a few old priests, left as a protection to the property of the villagers, and through their means we endeavoured to persuade the people to escape from their oppressors; but either from fear, or an idea that we must ultimately yield to the numerous legions of their king, and be forced to re-embark, our invitations at this time produced a very partial effect, even among those whose condition was the most wretched. A few families, however, were released from their guards by the sudden and unexpected arrival of the troops. These gladly chose to proceed to Rangoon; and to the influence of their report, of the kind treatment they experienced, we were subsequently indebted for the return of the great body of the people, to whose services and exertions the army was so much indebted in the ensuing campaign.

CHAPTER 6

The Attack at Syriam

The events of the month of July were followed by several important results, opening, for a time, a wider field to our foraging parties, enabling a few of the inhabitants to return to their homes, and obliging the enemy to draw their reinforcements from the more distant parts of the country. For some time after the expedition landed at Rangoon the warlike character and natural courage of the people, with their habits of implicit obedience to their chiefs, enabled the government to raise sufficient levies from the provinces immediately contiguous to the seat of war: but the case was now different; a serious impression had already been made upon the men of that part of the kingdom, who were no longer forward or desirous of serving, but downcast and dejected, with the remembrance: of their recent losses, and requiring the utmost vigilance and authority of their chiefs to keep them together. Desertion to a considerable extent had already taken place, and could only be kept in check by the most cruel measures, to which the Burmhan chiefs in such cases never fail to resort. To inspire confidence among the people, and to keep title generals and chiefs strictly to their duty, the Princes of Tonghoo and Sarrawaddy, brothers to the king, were ordered down from Ava, to superintend the operations of the War.

The first established his headquarters near Pegu, and the latter at Donoobew, upon the great river, about sixty miles from Rangoon, which had been fortified as a post of reserve and depot for the army, and no trouble was spared to render it in every respect a place of strength. On the arrival of the Princes at their posts, rigorous conscription laws were put in force, without producing much effect; orders were issued, threatening the most exemplary punishment to deserters, and such as were convicted of misconduct in the field, and promising liberal rewards and honours to all who might distinguish themselves in action with the enemy. They loudly proclaimed their intention of surrounding the British force, ordered the river in our rear to be blocked up; and, to insure success, these doughty warriors came accompanied by numerous astrologers, who were to fix upon the most favourable periods for carrying their plans into effect.

Blindly superstitious in some points, Burmese of all ranks implicitly believe in the predictions of these impostors. The influence of the moon upon the affairs of men is never doubted, and the calculations of the astrologers upon certain signs and indications of that planet obtain universal credit; from the fixing of a propitious time for attacking a position, to the most ordinary affair of life, nothing can prosper without consulting an astrologer; these men are consequently found in every corner of the kingdom, and are held in the highest esteem and veneration by the people. By persons of rank especially, these oracles are much favoured and respected, consulting them in all military operations, and abiding rigidly by their decisions. Their predictions on some occasions, however, were productive of more evil than good to the cause they wished to serve; for although they seldom failed to inspire the troops with a degree of confidence, the publicity that attended their decisions not infrequently found its way into our lines, and prepared us for the attack.

Another novel and formidable reinforcement about this time joined the enemy from Ava, styled the King's Invulnerables. This corps consists of several thousand men, divided, however, into many classes of warriors, of whom a select band only are specially entitled to the above-mentioned appellation. They are distinguished by the short cut of their hair, and the peculiar manner in which they are tattooed, having the figures of elephants, tigers, and a great variety of ferocious animals indelibly, and even beautifully, marked upon their arms and legs; but to the soldiers they were best known by having bits of gold, silver, and sometimes precious stones in their arms, probably introduced under the skin at an early age.

These men are considered by their countrymen as invulnerable; and from their foolish and absurd exposure of their persons to the fire of an enemy, they are either impressed with the same opinion, or find it necessary to show a marked contempt for danger in support of their pretensions. In all the stockades and defences of the enemy, one or two of these heroes were generally found, whose duty it was to exhibit the war-dance of defiance upon the most exposed part of their defences, infusing courage and enthusiasm into the minds of their comrades, and affording much amusement to their enemies. The infatuated wretches, under the excitement of opium, too frequently continued the ludicrous exhibition, till they afforded convincing proof of the value of their claims to the title they assume.

Great expectations were formed from the presence of the princes with the army, aided by astrology, and the united skill and valour of the sages and warriors, who had sworn to rid their country of its hostile intruders. As, however, a considerable period had to elapse from their arrival to the first predicted lucky moon, (of which due information was received at Rangoon,) when a nocturnal attack upon our lines was meditated, the interval was not allowed to pass unprofitably on our part.

At the mouth of the Pegu river, a little above its junction with that of Rangoon, and a few miles distant from the town, are the remains of the old Portuguese fort and factory of Syriam, built upon an eligible and commanding height, but, at the time we visited it, so completely overgrown with trees and brushwood, as to be scarcely perceptible from the river. In the beginning of August, this naturally strong post was occupied by a considerable force, with strict orders from the arrogant and ignorant Prince of Sarrawaddy, to block up the channel of the river in our rear, that not one of the "captive strangers" might escape the punishment that was about to overtake them.

The success which had attended the predatory excursions of this corps, in carrying off the boats of the fleet, and in preventing the fishermen from prosecuting their trade, at a time when our crowded hospitals, scantily provided with fresh meat, made a regular supply of fish an object of the greatest importance. These and other considerations rendered it expedient to drive the enemy to a more convenient distance from our lines; and on the morning of the 4th, a detachment, consisting of part of the forty-first regiment, the Company's Madras European regiment, and twelfth Madras native infantry, under Brigadier Smelt, was embarked in the flotilla for that purpose, proceeding to Syriam with the first of the tide. On landing, and penetrating a short distance through the brushwood, the old fort became visible, scarped, cleared, and prepared for our reception; the old wall, wherever it had given way, either renewed or covered by stockading; and huge beams of wood were suspended from the parapet, intended to be cut away, for the purpose of crushing both the scaling-ladders and those who might have the hardihood to attempt to place them.

Other obstacles had, however, to be overcome before the troops could come in contact with the enemy; a deep and impassable creek arresting their progress, when within musket-shot of the place. A party of sailors from His Majesty's ship *Lame*, under Captain Marryat, who accompanied the column, with the characteristic coolness and activity of British seamen, soon remedied the defect, and in a very short space of time a bridge was prepared, which enabled the column to push on to the point of attack; but neither the enemy's numerical superiority, nor their formidable preparations, had confirmed them in their purpose of steady resistance. While the troops were marching forward, a constant fire of artillery and musketry was indeed kept up; but no sooner had they gained the ramparts, than all resistance ceased, and the place, with eight guns, and a considerable quantity of ammunition, was quietly taken possession of.

Upon quitting the fort, the enemy retired upon ,the Pagoda of Syriam, pursued by a part of the detachment, along the narrow winding footpaths of the forest. On reaching the Pagoda, it was also found strongly occupied, with cannon pointing down every approach towards it from the jungle; and, like most buildings of the same description, standing on a hill, surrounded by a wall, and accessible only by the regular flights of stairs which lead to the interior: these also were strongly barricaded and otherwise defended. The column marched directly forward to the stairs, and had even partly ascended them before a shot was fired, the Burmese standing at their guns, coolly awaiting the approach; but when at length the firing did commence, the soldiers, pushing briskly forward, soon closed upon the enemy, who, probably disheartened by the presence of their comrades, who, had fled from the lower fort, showed less anxiety to defend their post, than to save themselves from actual collision with a force, represented, no doubt, as irresistible, by those whose ill success and shameful precipitation required an apology, and whose fears magnified the numbers of their enemy to an alarming degree.

Similar attacks were made with equal success upon different posts occupied by the enemy in the course of the month; one, in particular, upon a succession of stockades, situated on the Dalla river, cost us a considerable number of brave men; but, as scarcely a week elapsed in which detachments of the army were not employed upon this harassing and indispensable war of posts, varying little in circumstances from those already described, it would be tedious and superfluous to give a minute detail of each affair as they successively occurred.

Some weeks elapsed after the Prince of Sarrawaddy's arrival in the lower provinces, before the astrologers in his train could fix upon a propitious day for attacking our position; but at length intimation was received from prisoners who were taken, that the first lucky moon, as they styled it, would occur on the 30th and 31st of August, and that a body of the King's Invulnerables had promised to attack and carry the great Pagoda on one of these nights, that the prince and the pious men who accompanied him might celebrate the usual annual festival in that sacred place.

At midnight, on the 30th, the attempt was accordingly made, The Invulnerables, armed with swords and muskets, rushing in a compact body from the jungle under the Pagoda; a small piquet, thrown out in our front, retiring in slow and steady order, skirmishing with the head of the advancing column, until it reached the stairs leading up to the Pagoda, at the summit of which the troops were drawn out, silently awaiting the approach of The Invulnerables, whose numbers in the darkness of the night (the moon having set previous to the commencement of the attack) could only be guessed at, by the noise and clamour of their threats and imprecations upon the impious strangers, if they did not immediately evacuate the sacred temple, as, guided by a few glimmering lanterns in their front, they boldly and rapidly advanced in a dense multitude along the narrow pathway leading to the northern gateway. At length vivid flashes, followed by the cannon's thundering peals, broke from the silent ramparts of the British post, stilling the tumult of the advancing mass, while showers of grape and successive volleys of musketry fell with dreadful havoc among their crowded ranks, against which the imaginary shield of self-deceit and imposition was found of no avail, leaving the unfortunate Invulnerables scarcely a chance between destruction and inglorious flight. Nor did they hesitate long upon the alternative: a few devoted enthusiasts may have despised to fly, but as they all belonged to the same high-favoured caste, and had brought none of their less-favoured countrymen to witness their disgrace, the great body of them soon sought for safety ill the jungle, where they, no doubt, invented a plausible account of their night's adventure, which, however effectual it may have proved in saving their credit, had also the good effect to us of preventing them in future from volunteering upon such desperate services, and contributed, in some degree, to protect the troops from being so frequently deprived of their night's rest.

CHAPTER 7

The Retreat from Arracan

The time had now arrived when the disasters and defeats of three months, with the hopeless condition of the Burmese army at Rangoon, could no longer be concealed: wongees and princes had successively assumed the superintendance of the war, proclaiming to the King and the nation the approaching destruction of the British force, and had each in turn atoned for their loudly-vaunted threats of driving the invaders back into the ocean, by the conspicuous failure of their plans and operations, and the signal defeat of their feeble efforts to compel us to retire.

Supersession and disgrace had rapidly followed each other, through a long list of commanders, in the vain hope that one would at last be found possessed of sufficient talent to turn the tide of war on that side, where not only numbers, but, as they still boasted, valour also lay; and it was not until the catalogue of these heroes was expended, that his Burmhan Majesty turned his eyes to one then distant, at the head of his veteran legions, who had long stood pre-eminently high as a warrior and statesman; and had been the means of adding to the Burmese empire some of the most valuable acquisitions of his present Majesty. Maha Bandoola, the chief above alluded to, had, some time before the expedition reached Rangoon, proceeded to take command of the Arracan army destined for the invasion of Bengal.

On arriving in Arracan, the Bandoola lost no time in

commencing offensive operations; a strong corps was expeditiously moved forward to Ramoo, by the roads which had· been secretly prepared through the jungle: this greatly superior force, after some skirmishing, surrounded and made a general attack upon the small British post before it could be reinforced by the troops advancing to its support; and although an honourable resistance was made by the defendants, they were borne down by numbers, and completely cut up. Some of the officers and Sepoys effected their escape, but great numbers fell into the hands of the enemy, by whom the European officers and many of the native soldiers were most barbarously put to death.

On receiving the news of this disaster, and of the great force of the enemy, the commanding officer, advancing to the support of the Ramoo party, retired to prepare for the defence of Chittagong itself, to which it was supposed the enemy would immediately advance.

Exaggerated reports of the strength and ferocity of the Burmese troops were soon in circulation, carrying alarm even to Calcutta, the very name of Burmhan spreading dread and terror among the native population. The peasants on the frontier fled in dismay from their villages; and every idle rumour was magnified so industriously by timid or designing people, that the native merchants of Calcutta were with difficulty persuaded to refrain from removing their families and property from under the very guns of Fort William. The Burmese, however, did not advance beyond Ramoo, but were employed in erecting stockades in that, neighbourhood, which Bandoola, no doubt, intended should form the basis of his forward movement on the return of the cold season, but from which he was long previously recalled from all thoughts of invasion, to the defence of his own country.

The presence of such a force upon our frontier at so short a distance from the capital was naturally regarded with some anxiety in Bengal; and although the rainy season afforded a temporary security against its inroads and aggressions, its removal, nevertheless, was anxiously desired. That important object was at length gained by the successful operations of the Rangoon army. An order from Ava recalled Bandoola, with his legions, to the Irrawaddy, and in the latter end of August he suddenly broke up from Ramoo, and retired from the Chittagong district.

Little is known of the march of this force through the provinces, and across the mountains of Arracan, to the Irrawaddy; a distance, by the shortest route, of upwards of two hundred miles, at a season of the year when none but Burmhans could have kept the field for a week, much less have attempted to pass the insalubrious jungles and pestilential marshes of Arracan, with rivers, arms of the sea and mountain-torrents opposing their progress at every step. By a Burmese, however, obstacles of this description are little regarded: half amphibious in his nature, he takes the water without fear or reluctance; he is besides always provided with a chopper, and expert in the construction of rafts where necessary—seldom encumbered with commissariat or equipage of any kind, and carrying a fortnight's rice in a bag slung across his shoulders, he is at all times ready to move at the first summons of his chiefs, who, when unembarrassed by the presence of an enemy, divide into parties for the greater celerity of movement and provisioning of the men, each pursuing his own route to the place of general rendezvous appointed by the chief commander. Such, on this occasion, seems to have been the plan followed by Bandoola; and without its being even suspected by our advanced posts, his army, in the course of one night, disappeared from Ramoo, leaving no trace of the route by which it had retired; not even a sick man was left behind: a considerable store of grain, that had no doubt been collected for the meditated advance into Bengal, was the only thing found in the evacuated stockades.

Information of the retreat from Arracan soon reached Rangoon, affording at last a hope of a general trial of strength with the Burmese army; a prospect which, in the immoveable state of the British force, could not fail to be hailed with satisfaction, as likely to produce a more decisive influence upon the war, than the partial affairs we had hitherto been engaged in.

The arrival of Maha Bandoola at Ava, where high honours were conferred upon him, and his appointment to the command of the army of Henzawaddy, were speedily communicated to the crestfallen levies in our frost; the very name of the new commander restoring confidence and courage, and acting as a spell in drawing forward the lately reluctant peasantry to range themselves under the banners of so popular a leader. The arrival of part of the Arracan force at Sembeughewn was soon afterwards made known, and different parties, which had marched along the sea-coast or crossed the mountains near to Prome, were gradually arriving at the general rendezvous at Donoobew. The Bandoola himself was to leave Ava with a large fleet of boats, containing a train of artillery, and to be joined by the several detachments on his progress down the river. The whole of this new army was to assemble in the neighbourhood of Donoobew, from which place it was supposed it would not move forward to join the levies in our front before November, when the rainy season would be over.

In the meantime the troops at Rangoon were not idle, nor did the British Commander allow the enemy any time to recover from the impression that had been made, and the panic that prevailed among them, No opportunity was lost of attacking every assailable point they occupied. Their stockades upon the Dalla river, and those upon the Panlaug branch or principal passage into the Irrawaddy, were attacked and carried with few casualties on our part, while the enemy in both instances suffered severely, with the additional loss of many pieces of artillery.

The rains continued during the whole month of September, and sickness had arrived at an alarming height. An epidemic fever, which prevailed all over India, made its appearance among the troops, which, although in few instances of a fatal tendency, left all those whom it attacked in a deplorable state of weakness and debility, accompanied by cramps, and pains in the limbs: men discharged from the hospitals were long in regaining their strength; and too frequently indulged in pineapples, limes, and other fruit with which the woods about Rangoon abound, bringing on dysentery, which, in their exhausted state, generally terminated in death.

The incessant rains, with severe and indispensable duty, no doubt added to the sickness; and although the climate is perhaps as favourable to Europeans as that of any part of our eastern possessions, they, in particular, suffered most severely, dying in great numbers daily.

Our situation at this time was, indeed, truly melancholy; even those who still continued to do their duty, emaciated and reduced, could with difficulty crawl about. The hospitals crowded, and with all the care and attention of a numerous and experienced medical staff, the sick for many months continued to increase, until scarcely three thousand duty-soldiers were left to guard the lines. Floating hospitals were established at the mouth of the river, bread was furnished in sufficient quantities, but nothing except change of season, or of climate, seemed likely to restore the sufferers to health.

Mergui and Tavoy now in our possession, and represented by the professional men who visited them as possessing every requisite advantage, were accordingly fixed on as convalescent stations. To these places numbers were subsequently sent, and the result fully justified the most sanguine expectations that were formed. Men who had for months remained in a most debilitated state at Rangoon, rapidly recovered on arriving at Mergui, and were soon restored in full health and vigour to their duty.

CHAPTER 8

The Fall of Martaban

The inveterate enmity and constant warfare existing between the Burmese and Siamese nations for some time encouraged an opinion, that the latter kingdom would not fail to assist in the attack upon the territories of their old enemy. The landing of the British at Rangoon opened to the court of Siam a favourable, and long-sought, opportunity of revenging the many humiliating defeats they had sustained from their more powerful and warlike neighbour, and of recovering their lost possessions on the coast of Tenasserim. Such an opportunity the Siamese government would no doubt have profited by, and not improbably may have contemplated the seizure of Mergui and Tavoy, when their reduction by the British not only deprived them of all hope of acquisition in that quarter, but probably alarmed their fears and jealousies at the approach of an European settlement putting a stop to their annual marauding excursions for the purpose of carrying off the unprotected peasantry of these provinces; and it may also be questioned, whether they did not regard the vicinity of a British force with greater alarm and jealousy than they would have felt at any successes of the Burmese.

Certain it is, the King of Ava did not neglect to awaken their alarm, urging his Siamese Majesty, by every consideration for their mutual security, to join his forces to those of Ava, in repelling an invasion, represented as having, for its object, the ruin and destruction of both countries. The

Siamese Monarch, however, thought proper to pursue a safer course, endeavouring to persuade both parties of his friendly disposition, and determination of taking an early part in the war, but cautiously abstaining from any decided hostility on either side.

That the Siamese were, till the very· last, convinced that we should fail in conquering Ava, or in bringing its government to sue for terms, there is abundant testimony, drawn both from their conduct, and the concurring observation of their measures at Bangkok, by the resident at that city; and the situation of their capital upon the coast, exposed to an attack by sea, probably alone prevented them from making common cause against us, in so far, at least, as using their utmost efforts to prevent a British settlement from being formed on the coast of Tenasserim, as an event in every respect alarming, and fraught with danger to themselves.

The risk, however, of a rupture with a strong maritime power was not to be hastily incurred; and the King of Siam contented himself with making a display of preparations for immediate war, while, in reality, he intended to maintain a strict neutrality, hoping, by skilful management, to reap some advantage to himself, whoever might come off as conquerors. From the British he might claim Tavoy, Martaban, or some other convenient portion of territory, as the reward of his pretended friendship and services, while he would not be displeased to see his old enemy somewhat humbled and curtailed in his possessions. Should the Burmese, an the other hand, succeed in forcing us to abandon our conquests, the Siamese could readily step into the conquered towns of Tenasserim, either as a gift from the British, or upon their leaving them before the arrival of a Burmhan force; and which, under some pretence or other, they would find the means of permanently retaining.

But, whatever might be the views of his Siamese Majesty, to convince, or deceive either party, it was necessary to act; and a body of his troops soon accordingly appeared upon the Martaban frontier, ready to take the field, either to attack Rangoon, or act in concert with the British, at the opening of the campaign, as circumstances, and the situation of the belligerents, might point out to be the safest policy a movement which, added to other considerations, determined the British general, early in October, to reduce and occupy the town of Martaban, from which a direct communication could be opened with the Siamese army, and their motions watched.

One chief cause of ancient feud and hatred between the Burmese and Siamese nations seems to have arisen from the latter having received and protected many families of Taliens, or Peguers, at the time their country was subdued and incorporated with Ava, and who, from rank or situation, were doomed to be put to death by the conquerors. These men, or their descendants, taking advantage of any favourable opportunity, might probably still have sufficient influence with their countrymen to induce them to revolt from their usurpers. Some dread of this nature, or the most insatiable thirst for conquest, can alone account for the steady perseverance of the court of Ava in its attacks upon Siam, carried on with an obstinacy and indifference to losses, that went far to prove they would never rest until their enemy was finally subdued.

The existence of such a people as a distinct race of Taliens, or of any branch of the ancient dynasty of Pegu in Siam, was to us a question of great importance, as affording, at any time, a much more permanent and less troublesome method of reducing the overgrown power of Ava, by the dismemberment of the empire, emancipating the southern provinces, and establishing the ancient kingdom of Pegu, should the persevering obstinacy of the King of Ava render such a measure indispensable in providing for the future quiet of the eastern world. Independent, however, of such considerations, having in our power an hereditary heir to the throne of Pegu might have some weight with his Burmhan Majesty in bringing him to terms.

The city of Martaban, situated at the bottom of the gulf of that name, and about a hundred miles to the eastward of Rangoon, had been long considered as a place of some note, both in a political and commercial point of view, as the capital and market of an extensive province, but more especially as a frontier fortress, and depot of military stores; where the Burmese armies were usually assembled, in their frequent wars with the Siamese, and from whence irruptions into the territories of the latter were annually made, under various pretences, for the sake of plunder, and in the hope of securing prisoners.

In a country thinly peopled, and whose inhabitants, from their military habits, are averse to work, the importance of such a prize as a long list of slaves may be conceived; and it appears to have been a chief desideratum with the Burmese in all their wars. A great proportion of the most valuable part of the inhabitants of the conquered countries being carried into captivity, numbers of these unfortunate beings from Cassay, Arracan, and Assam, are to be found in Ava.; and even villages are to be met with on the Irrawaddy, inhabited by mechanics, iron-smiths, and particular trades, whose features plainly indicate a foreign origin, although, in other respects, they are scarcely to be distinguished from the natives of the country.

The Muniporeans, or people of Cassay, in particular, abound in great numbers, and they are much prized as clever workmen. Owing to their superior skill in the management of the horse, the Burmese cavalry is almost exclusively composed of them; and they are distinguished by the national appellation of "The Cassay Horse."

On the frontiers of Martaban, a constant border warfare seems to have been carried on by the Burmese; but they were now either too seriously occupied at home to molest or interfere with their neighbours, or from some secret understanding, the Siamese troops were permitted to remain undisturbed within a few days' march of the city.

Such was the state of affairs at Martaban, when, on the 13th of October, the small force consisting of part of His Majesty's Forty-First Regiment, and the 3rd Madras Native Light Infantry, under Lieutenant-Colonel Godwin, sailed from Rangoon for that place. Owing to light and contrary winds, the expedition did not reach its destination so soon as was expected; and instead of taking the enemy by surprise, they found him fully aware of their approach, and that every preparation had been made for their reception. The governor, Maha Oudnah, a bold and resolute chief, had fortified with skill and labour every commanding eminence about the town, and its distance from the coast nearly twenty miles, offered many serious obstacles to the approach of our troops. By land, difficult forests, marshes, and extensive plains of rice-grounds, still covered with the inundations of the monsoon, prevented a movement from the coast in that way; while the intricate navigation of a shallow winding river presented many imped-iments to an ~approach by water. The latter course, however, was at once resolved on, and by toil and perseverance, the ves-sels were finally anchored nearly abreast of the town; and the governor evincing no disposition to come to terms, an assault took place, when the enemy was driven with severe loss from every part of his defences.

The inhabitants of Martaban, who are chiefly Taliens or Peguers received the British troops with every appearance of joy and satisfaction; and for a year and a half, that they were afterwards living under British protection, conducted themselves, on all occasions to the satisfaction of the British authorities, and even offered to make common cause against their Burmese conquerors. Martaban indeed, is the only prov-ince in Pegu where a strong and marked national antipathy was found to exist against the Burmese government.

The disappearance of every trace of the royal family of Pegu, the cruel policy of the conquerors in exterminating or driving into perpetual banishment every chief and man of weight, and their subsequent judicious system of amalgamation with the conquered, had well nigh obliterated all remembrance of ancient independence in most parts of the country; and if a feeling of regret has survived that crisis when the very name of Peguer was proscribed, it is only to be found among the Taliens of Martaban, or remembered as a dream by the descendants of the persecuted families who fled into Siam.

In Pegu itself no such feeling certainly exists; the invariably adopted system of the court of Ava, already alluded to, and its judicious treatment of the conquered, has long since removed every appearance of distinction between Burmese and Peguer. No invidious preference is ever shown; all enjoy equal rights and privileges, and both are equally eligible to fill the highest posts under government. That the people of the lower provinces, generally, after experiencing the mild and equitable sway of an enlightened government, should have been actuated by the strongest desire to be released from the iron sceptre which had so long ruled them, cannot be wondered at; and that they were ready and anxious to go any length to gain so desirable an object, many proofs were given; but the desire, except in some few instances, cannot be ascribed to any distinct national feeling or wish to regain an independence, the very remembrance of which had passed away.

After arranging matters at Martaban, the Lieutenant-Colonel detached a party against Yeh, situated to the eastward between Martaban and Tavoy, which fell into our hands without resistance.

CHAPTER 9

The Burmese Prepare to Attack

By the end of October the rains had ceased; and the return of the cold season, at all times so ardently hailed with pleasure in warm climates, could not fail to receive a double welcome from men who had for five months experienced so much misery and inconvenience, exposed to severe and arduous duty before an enemy, at a season of the year when the troops of all other nations than those of Ava would have permitted us to enjoy uninterrupted rest—the soldiers naturally ascribing· their sufferings, and much of the sickness that had prevailed among them, to the baneful influence and long continuance of the monsoon.

It however proved, as it generally does, in countries subject to periodical rains, that the most unhealthy period is that which immediately follows their termination; when the unwholesome exhalations from the ground, and noxious vapours from sheets of stagnant water, are pregnant with disease and death.

This was felt to be particularly the case at Rangoon; and in October, the sickness and number of deaths were greater than in any previous month. In November, however, a sensible change in the health of the troops was apparent; and although their numbers were by that time woefully reduced, it was gratifying to observe the men out of the hospitals gradually regaining that state of health and strength so requisite for undergoing the duties of active service, while their spirits, which had remained firm and unsubdued in the midst of trials of no ordinary magnitude, rose with the prospect of an early meeting with the enemy, of a nature more consonant to the feelings and character of a British soldier, than the indecisive and harassing warfare they had lately been engaged in.

The promise, too, of an early movement in advance, and the consequent change of scene, so pleasing and exhilarating to men who have suffered from the effects of climate, had its influence, even upon the hospitals, in awakening the unfortunate sufferers from the lethargy of debility and causing a most anxious desire in all, to be able to join their comrades in the approaching operations. But the time was still distant when any forward movement could be anticipated.

The whole force of Ava advancing upon Rangoon must previously be disposed of and even if successful in defeating that force, and overturning the formidable preparations in array against us, there was but too great reason to fear that our numbers would be so much reduced as to forbid the prosecution of offensive operations, while, up to the end of November, we were still unprovided with the means of moving a single company. Measures, however, were in train for supplying, as far as possible, the wants of the army; and the presidencies of Calcutta and Fort St. George were using every effort to equip the force, as far as the partial means at their immediate disposal would permit.

The reduction of all the enemy's maritime possessions had now been accomplished; his armies had been defeated at every point without producing any of the results which had been calculated on; and it could no longer be presumed as even probable, that the defeat of Bandoola's force would be attended with any more permanent or decisive advantages, or incline the court of Ava to sue for peace. The obstinate, blind, and arrogant character of that government became daily more conspicuous; their resources and determination had already greatly surpassed all previous calculation; and while the British army remained stationary, it was but too obvious they would neither want men, means, nor inclination to prolong the contest, already sufficiently ruinous in expense and waste of lives.

A decided forward movement, at least to Prome, or even the reduction of the capital, might still be necessary to bring the infatuated Monarch to his senses; and brief as the season of preparation must necessarily be, every possible exertion was made to enable a small corps to make the effort after the trial of strength had taken place, which the enemy was so kindly preparing to accommodate us with on our own ground.

From the best information we could receive, the country would not be in a state to enable the troops to march, with safety to their health, before the end of January; up to the middle of November it was still covered with water, and even the Bandoola's army had to come to the scene of action chiefly by water. Five hundred Mug boatmen had arrived from Chittagong, and were busily engaged in preparing boats for river service; and a reinforcement of two British regiments, the First and Forty-Seventh; some battalions of native infantry; a regiment of cavalry; a troop of horse-artillery and one of rockets, were also destined to join the army before it moved in advance. Already transports with draught cattle were beginning to arrive: officers and men were engaged in preparing far the march, when our attention was summoned to our front by the near approach of Maha Bandoola and his army.

The efforts of the last three months spent in collecting and organizing the military resources of the nation, and the arrival of the troops from Arracan, in the beginning of November, had placed that favourite leader at the head of sixty thousand fighting men, with a considerable train of artillery and a body of Cassay horse. The several corps and detachments, proceeding from many different parts of the empire, were by that time assembled, and in readiness to move from Donoobew, the place of general meeting, where they had been joined by the Bandoola, and several other chiefs of rank and reputation.

This army was esteemed the largest and best armed the court of Ava had ever sent into the field; and unbounded expectations of success were entertained from its vast numerical superiority over the British, and from the vaunting confidence and high character of its general.

The musketeers were estimated at thirty-five thousand men; great numbers were armed with jingals, a small but most annoying piece, carrying a ball of from six to twelve ounces, and mounted on a carriage which two men can manage and move about at pleasure. The Cassay horse amounted to seven hundred, and a considerable body of men was attached to the guns, which were carried from the river to the scene of action on elephants' backs. The rest of the force was armed with swords and spears, and well provided with the necessary implements for stockading and entrenching. This last class are attached to, and act in concert with the musketeers, by whose fire they are covered when employed in sapping or making their approaches upon a defending enemy, mutually supporting each other in every situation. in their close engagements of stockaded warfare, these spearmen are far from being the least formidable of the Burmhan troops; endowed by nature with great physical strength, their long spears and short swords give them an advantage at close quarters even over the musket and bayonet. But the force would not have been complete without the addition of Invulnerables, who, amply provided with charms, spells, and opium, in the ensuing operations afforded much amusement in the dance of defiance, committing all manner of ludicrous extravagances, with the most prodigal exposure of their persons.

Confused rumours of the arrival of the Arracan army on the Irrawaddy at Sembeugheuwn and other points, and of its junction with other levies and corps on its way down the river; of their concentration at Donoobew, and the movement of successive divisions towards our front; and finally of Bandoola's approach with the main body of his grand army, reached Rangoon early in November: but such vigilance and alert watch was still maintained by the disheartened legions in our neighbourhood, now almost dwindled into a military police, that no correct information could be obtained either of the strength or movements of the advancing army; and it was not until towards the end of the month, that full and authentic information was obtained by means of an intercepted despatch from Bandoola to the ex-governor of Martaban, in which he notified his having left Prome at the head of an invincible army, with horses and elephants, and all manner of warlike stores for the purpose of capturing or expelling the English from Rangoon.

The intelligence was no sooner received than every necessary arrangement was made for the Bandoola's reception. The Eighty-Ninth regiment had rejoined from Tavoy, but our diminished numbers were still very inadequate to the defence of the extensive position (as has been already mentioned) we had unavoidably to occupy. To remedy, however, this evil as far as possible, posts, consisting of redoubts and fortified pagodas, well defended by artillery, and held by small garrisons, were speedily constructed, connecting the great pagoda by two distinct lines, one fronting to the east, and the other to the west, with Rangoon and the river—leaving a disposable force for moving to the support of any point, or for attacking the enemy, should he afford an opportunity of doing so to advantage.

The post at Kemmendine was also strongly occupied, and supported on the river by His Majesty's sloop, *Sophie*, Captain Ryves, a Company's cruiser, and a strong division of gunboats: this post was of great importance in preventing the enemy from attacking Rangoon by water, or launching from a convenient distance the numerous formidable fire-rafts he had prepared for the destruction of our shipping.

On the 30th of November the Burmese army was assembled in the extensive forest in front of the Shoedagon pagoda, and his line extending from the river above Kemmendine in a semicircular direction towards Puzendown, might be distinguished by a curved line of smoke rising above the trees from the bivouacs of the different corps. During the following night the low, continued murmur and hum of voices proceeding from the enemy's encampment suddenly ceased, and was speedily succeeded by the distant but gradually approaching sounds of a multitude in slow and silent movement through the woods; and we soon became aware that, the enemy's masses had approached to the very edge of the jungle, within musket-shot of the pagoda, apparently in readiness to rush from their cover to the assault at the break of day.

Towards morning, however, the woods resounded with the blows of the falling-axe and hammer, and with the crash of falling trees, leaving us for some time in doubt whether or not the noise was intended as a *ruse* to draw our attention from the front, or whether the Burmese commanders had resolved to proceed with their usual slow, safe, and systematic measures of attack.

CHAPTER 10

The Great Assault

The day had scarcely dawned, on the 1st of December, when hostilities commenced with a heavy fire of musketry and cannon at Kemmendine, the reduction of that place being a preliminary to any general attack upon our line. The firing continued long and animated; and from our commanding situation at the Great Pagoda, though nearly two miles distant from the scene of action, we could distinctly hear the yells and shouts of the infuriated assailants, occasionally returned by the hearty cheer of the British seamen, as they poured in their heavy broadsides upon the resolute and persevering masses. The thick forest which separated us from the river, prevented our seeing distinctly what was going forward; and when the firing ceased, we remained for a short time in some anxiety, though in little doubt as to the result of the long and spirited assault.

At length, however, the thick canopy of smoke, which lowered over the fierce and sanguinary conflict, gradually dissolving, we had the pleasure of seeing the masts of our vessels lying at their old station off the fort—a convincing proof that all had ended well on our side.

In the course of the forenoon Burmese columns were observed on the west side of the river, marching across the plain of Dalla, towards Rangoon. They were formed in five or six different divisions, and moved with great regularity, led by numerous chiefs on horseback—their gilt umbrellas glittering in the rays of the sun, with a sufficiently formidable and imposing effect, at a distance that prevented our perceiving anything motley or mobbish, which might have been found in a closer inspection of these warlike legions. On reaching the bank of the river opposite to Rangoon, the men of the leading division, laying aside their arms, commenced entrenching and throwing up batteries for the destruction of the shipping, while the main body disappeared in a jungle ·in the rear, where they began stockading and establishing their camp, gradually reinforcing the front line as the increasing extent of the batteries and entrenchments permitted.

Later in the day, several heavy columns were observed issuing from the forest, about a mile in front of the east face of the Great Pagoda, with flags and banners flying in profusion. Their march was directed along a gently-sloping woody ridge towards Rangoon: the different corps successively taking up their ground along the ridge, soon assumed the appearance of a complete line, extending from the forest in front of the Pagoda, to within long gun-shot distance of the town, and resting on the river at Puzendown, which was strongly occupied by cavalry and infantry; these formed the left wing of the Burmese army.

The centre, or the continuation of the line, from the Great Pagoda up to Kemmendine, where it again rested on the river, was posted in so thick a forest, as to defy all conjecture as to its strength or situation; but we were well aware that the principal force occupied the jungle in the immediate vicinity of the pagoda, which was naturally considered as the key to our position, and upon which the great effort would accordingly be made. In the course of a few hours we thus found ourselves completely surrounded, with the narrow· channel of the Rangoon river alone unoccupied in our rear, and with only the limited space within our lines that we could still call our own.

The line of circumvallation taken up by the enemy, obviously extended a very considerable distance, and divided as it was by the river, injudiciously weakened his means of assailing us on any particular point; but as far as celerity, order, and regularity are concerned, the style in which the different corps took up their stations in the line, reflected much credit on the arrangement of the Burmese commander. When this singular and presumptuous formation was completed, the soldiers of the left columns also laying aside their spears and muskets, commenced operations with their entrenching tools, with such activity and good will, that in the course of a couple of hours their line had wholly disappeared, and could only be traced by a parapet of new earth gradually increasing in height, and assuming such forms as the skill and science of the engineer suggested. The moving masses, which had so very lately attracted our anxious attention, had sunk into the ground; and to anyone who had not witnessed the whole scene, the existence of these subterranean legions would not have been credited: the occasional movement of a chief, with his gilt chattah (umbrella), from place to place, superintending the progress of their labour, was the only thing that now attracted notice. By a distant observer, the hills, covered with mounds of earth, would have been taken for anything rather than the approaches of an attacking army; but to us who had watched the whole strange proceeding, it seemed the work of magic or enchantment.

In the afternoon His Majesty's Thirteenth Regiment and the Eighteenth Madras Native Infantry, under Major Sale, were ordered to move rapidly forward upon the busily-employed and too-confident enemy; and as was suspected, they were found wholly unprepared for such a visit, or for our acting in any way, against such numerous opponents, on the offensive. They had scarcely perceived the approach of our troops before they were upon them, and the fire which they at last commenced proved wholly inadequate to checking their advance.. Having forced a passage through the entrenchments and taken the enemy in flank, the British detachment drove the whole line from their cover with considerable loss;

and having destroyed as many of their arms and tools as they could find, retired unmolested before the numerous bodies which were now forming on every side around them.

The trenches were found to be a succession of holes, capable of containing two men each, and excavated, so as to afford shelter, both from the weather and the fire of an enemy; even a shell lighting in the trench could at most but kill two men. As it is not the Burmese system to relieve their troops in making these approaches, each hole contained a sufficient supply of rice, water, and even fuel for its inmates; and under the excavated bank, a bed of straw or brushwood was prepared, in which one man could sleep while his comrade watched. When one line of trench is completed, its occupiers, taking advantage of the night, push forward to where the second line is to be opened, their place being immediately taken up by fresh troops from the rear, and so on progressively—the number of trenches occupied varying according to the force of the besiegers, to the plans of the general, or to the nature of the ground.

The Burmese, in the course of the evening, re-occupied their trenches, and re-commenced their labours, as if nothing had occurred; their commander, however, took the precaution of bringing forward a strong corps of reserve to the verge of the forest, from which his left, wing had issued, to protect it from any future interruption in its operations.

During the day, repeated attacks on Kemmendine had been made and repulsed; but it was not until darkness had set in, that the last desperate effort of the day was made to gain possession of that post. Already the wearied soldier; had lain down to rest, when suddenly the heavens and the whole surrounding country became brilliantly illuminated by the flames of several tremendous fire-rafts, floating down the river towards Rangoon; and scarcely had the blaze appeared, when incessant rolls of musketry and peals of cannon were heard from Kemmendine. The enemy had launched their fire-rafts into the stream with the first of the ebb tide, in the hope of driving the vessels from their stations off the place; and they were followed up by war-boats ready to take advantage of the confusion which might ensue, should any of them be set on fire. The skill and intrepidity of British seamen, however, proved more than a match for the numbers and devices of the enemy: entering their boats they grappled the flaming rafts, and conducted them past the shipping, or ran them ashore upon the bank.

On the land side the enemy were equally unsuccessful, being again repulsed with heavy loss, in the most resolute attempt they had yet made to reach the interior of the fort. The fire-rafts were, upon examination, found to be ingeniously contrived, and formidably constructed, made wholly of bamboos firmly wrought together, between every two or three rows of which a line of earthen jars of considerable size, filled with petroleum, or earth-oil and cotton, were secured; other inflammable ingredients were also distributed in different parts of the raft, and the almost inextinguishable fierceness of the flames proceeding from them can scarcely be imagined. Many of them were considerably upwards of a hundred feet in length, and were divided into many pieces attached to each other by means of long hinges, so arranged, that when they caught upon the cable or bow of any ship, the force of the current would carry the ends of the raft completely round her, and envelope her in flames from the deck to her main-topmast head, with scarcely a possibility of extricating herself from the devouring element.

With possession of Kemmendine, the enemy could have launched these rafts into the stream, from a point where they must have reached our shipping in the crowded harbour, but while we retained that post, they were obliged to despatch them from above it, and the setting of the current carried them, after passing the vessels at the station, upon a projecting point of land, where they almost invariably grounded; and this circumstance, no doubt, much increased Bandoola's anxiety to drive us from so important a position.

At daylight, on the morning of the 2nd, the enemy were observed still busily at work on every part of their line, and to have completely entrenched themselves upon some high and open ground, within musket-shot distance of the north face of the Great Pagoda, from which it was also separated by a considerable tank, named by the Rangoon settlers, (probably on account of the sulphurous qualities of its water,) the Scotch tank. Upon this ridge, and a woody valley to its right, frequent skirmishing now took place; and on several occasions it became necessary to dislodge them from particular points, from which their guns could enfilade our line, or their musketry be brought to bear upon the very barracks occupied by our soldiers, in which they were now not infrequently wounded while asleep.

In the spirited encounters which the enemy's near approach gave rise to, it was gratifying to observe the undaunted bearing of the British soldier, in the midst of countless numbers of the enemy, who were not to be driven from their ground by the united fire of musketry and cannon.

In the imagined safety of their cover they firmly maintained themselves, and returned our fire; and it was only at the decisive and intrepid charge, that they quailed to the courage of the European, and refused to meet him hand to hand.

During the 3rd and 4th, the enemy continued their approaches upon every part of our position with indefatigable labour and assiduity. At the Great Pagoda they had now reached the margin of the tank, and kept up a constant fire upon our barracks, saluting with a dozen muskets every one who showed his head above the ramparts, and, when nothing better could be done, expending both round and grape shot in vain attempts to strike the British ensign, which proudly waved high upon their sacred temple. On the side of Rangoon, they had approached near enough to fire an occasional gun upon the town, while they maintained incessant warfare with two small posts in its front, to which they were now so near, as to keep their garrisons constantly on the alert, in expectation of being attacked. From the entrenchments on the opposite side of the river, an incessant fire was kept up day and night upon our shipping, which were all anchored as near as possible to the Rangoon side, with the exception of one or two armed vessels, which still kept the middle of the stream, and returned the enemy's fire.

At Kemmendine, peace was seldom maintained above two hours at any time; but the little garrison (composed of the Twenty-Sixth Madras Native Infantry and a European detachment), though worn out with fatigue and want of rest, undauntedly received, and successfully repulsed, every successive attack of the enemy's fresh troops. The Sepoys, with unwearied constancy and the noblest feeling, even declined leaving their post, or laying aside their muskets for the purpose of cooking, lest it should give an advantage to the enemy, and contented themselves for several days with little else than dry rice for food.

On the river, the situation of the vessels was often extremely perilous: some of them were occasionally forced to slip their cables, and on one occasion the *Teignmouth* cruiser actually caught fire, which was with difficulty extinguished; but British seamanship finally triumphed over every device of the crafty and ingenious enemy, who, fertile as they had shown themselves in expedient, and confidently as they had commenced their operations, at last began to slacken in their efforts, and gradually became less vigorous in the obstinate and protracted contest for the possession of the post.

The materiel and warlike stores of the enemy's left wing being now brought forward from the jungle to their entrenchments, and completely within our reach, and their threatening vicinity to the town creating some uneasiness for the safety of our military stores, which were all lodged in that ill-protected and highly-combustible assemblage of huts and wooden-houses, the British general determined to make a decisive attack upon that part of the opposing army; and on the morning of the 5th, two columns of attack, consisting of detachments from different regiments, were for that purpose formed, one eight hundred strong, under Major Sale, of the 13th regiment, and the other of five hundred, under Major Walker, of the Madras army.

Major Sale was directed to attack the centre of the enemy's line, and Major Walker to advance from the post in front of the town, and to attack vigorously on that side; and a troop of dragoons, which had only been landed on the preceding day, was added to the first column, ready to take advantage of the enemy's retreat across the open ground to the jungle.

Early on that morning, as previously arranged, the naval commander, Captain Chads, proceeded up the Puzendown Creek, within gun-shot of the rear of the enemy's line, with the man-of-war boats and part of the flotilla, and commenced a heavy cannonade upon the nearest entrenchments, attracting the enemy's chief attention to that point, until the pre-concerted signal for attack was made, when both columns moved off together; but from some obstacle in the ground, Major Walker's party first reached its destined point, and made a spirited assault upon the lines. The enemy made a good resistance, and Major Walker, and many of his gallant comrades, fell in the advance to the first entrenchment, which was finally carried at the point of the bayonet, and the enemy successively driven from trench to trench, till this part of the field presented the appearance of a total rout.

The other column now commencing its attack in front, quickly forced the centre, and the whole Burmese left wing, entrenched upon the plain, was broken and dispersed, flying in hundreds, or assembling in confused and detached parties, or else maintaining a useless and disjointed resistance from different parts of the works to which our troops had not yet penetrated. The two British columns now forming a junction, pursued, and drove the defendants from every part of their works into the jungle, leaving the ground behind them covered with dead and wounded, with all their guns, entrenching tools, and a great number of small-arms; while the judgment, celerity, and spirit with which the attack was made had taken the enemy so entirely unawares, that our troops suffered comparatively trifling loss.

The 6th was spent by the Bandoola in rallying his defeated left; but it appeared to be still far from his intention to give up the contest on account of the failures and defeats he had already sustained. In front of the Great Pagoda, his troops still laboured with unabated zeal in their approaches upon our position; and this part of his line had been strongly reinforced by the troops which had been driven from the plain on the preceding day.

The morning of the 7th was fixed upon for bringing matters to a crisis at this point; and four columns of attack, composed of detachments, were early formed, under the superintendence of the commander of the forces, in readiness to move from the Pagoda, and assail the entrenchments on both flanks, and in the centre. Before the troops advanced, a severe cannonade was opened from many pieces of heavy ordnance, which had been brought up from the river, and placed in battery for the defence of this important post. This the enemy stood with much firmness, and returned it, with a constant, though very unequal, fire of musketry, jingals, and light artillery.

While the firing continued, the columns of attack were already in motion towards their several points; and when it ceased, the left corps, under Colonel Mallet, was seen debouching from the jungle upon the enemy's right; the right column under Colonel Brodie, Madras army, in like manner advancing on the left; and the two central columns, one under Colonel Parlby, of the Madras army, the other commanded by Captain Wilson, of His Majesty's Thirty-Eighth Regiment, descending the stairs from the north gate of the Pagoda, and filing up towards the centre of the position by either side of the tank formerly mentioned, as partly covering the entrenchments on this side. The appearance of our troops at the same moment upon so many different points seemed to paralyze their opponents; but they soon recovered from their momentary panic, and opened a hearty and well sustained fire upon the assailants; and it was not until a decided charge was made, and our troops actually in the trenches, that the enemy finally gave way: their courage failed them at this extremity, and they were precipitately driven from their numerous works, curiously shaped, and strengthened by man; strange contrivances, into the thick forest in their rear.

Here all pursuit was necessarily given up; our limited numbers, exhausted by seven days of watching and hard service, were unequal to further fatigue; though even when our men were fresh, the enemy could at all times baffle their pursuit in a country which to them afforded so many facilities for escaping.

Upon the ground, the enemy left a great number of dead, who seemed generally, from their stout and athletic forms, to have been their best troops. Their bodies had each a charm of some description, in which the brave deceased had no doubt trusted for protection against all harm and every danger, although on this occasion they seemed to have completely lost their virtue. In the entrenchments scaling ladders were found, and everything in readiness for storming the Pagoda.

No time was now lost in completing the: defeat of the Burmese army; and on the evening of the 7th, a body of troops, from His Majesty's Eighty-Ninth Regiment, and the Forty-Third Madras Native Infantry, under Colonel Parlby, were in readiness to embark from Rangoon as soon as the tide served, for the purpose of crossing the river and driving the enemy from their entrenchments at Dalla. The night was fortunately dark, and the troops landed unobserved upon the opposite shore. Not a shot was fired, nor alarm given, until the British soldiers had actually entered the entrenchments, and began firing at random upon the noisy groups, which were now heard on every side around them; but the danger of firing upon one another soon rendered it expedient to desist. Parties were sent to occupy different parts of the works, which previous acquaintance with the ground, enabled them to accomplish with trifling loss or opposition; and at daylight next morning they found themselves in full and quiet possession of the whole position with all the guns and stores of this part of the: army; and the enemy were seen during the whole day retracing their steps across the plain of Dalla much more expeditiously and with much less pomp and regularity than they had displayed in traversing it seven days before.

The: Burmese loss in killed and wounded during the operations must have been very great; but their invariable practice of removing their dead on all occasions when it can be done, and the immediate vicinity of a thick forest to the scene of all the engagements, affording in the present instance every .facility for so doing, it was difficult to form any correct estimate of the extent of their losses before Rangoon. They, however, left a sufficient number of dead upon the ground to show that they had suffered most severely; and what was perhaps of still more consequence to them than the lives of men they placed so little value on, every gun they had, and the whole materiel of their army, was captured and remained in our possession.

Numerous desertions, and even the dispersion of entire corps, followed the defeat of the Burmese army; and in the course of a few days the haughty Bandoola, who had been so lavish of his vaunts and threats of punishing the rebel strangers, found himself foiled in his plans, humbled and disappointed in all his expectations, and surrounded by the mere beaten and disheartened remnant of his invincible army, alike afraid of the consequences of a final retreat and of another meeting with his adversaries.

CHAPTER 11

Fire!

On the morning of the 9th, the vast multitude which had so long surrounded us had wholly disappeared; the Bandoola, with the veteran band which still adhered to him, retiring from the field of his disasters towards Donoobew, now strongly· fortified, and ready for his reception. He had not, however, proceeded far in his retreat, when he was met by considerable reinforcements, and shame and dread of the consequences of a tyrant's disappointment, acting at once upon a mind naturally bold and daring, he resolved to make a last and desperate effort to retrieve his blighted fame, and to afford the British force the opportunity of making their victory, and his disgrace complete.

During the seven days' operations at Rangoon; a corps of reserve posted at the village of Kokeen, distant four miles from the Great Pagoda, and where the Burmese headquarters were established, were busily employed upon an extensive field-work which had been marked out along an elevated ridge, that commanded the road leading from Rangoon towards the enemy's line of river defences, up to Donoobew. To this position the Bandoola now returned, and his force, reduced to less than twenty-five thousand men, recommenced its labours in fortifying the ground, with an activity and assiduity that Burmese troops alone are capable of.

The height was, in an incredibly short space of time, completely stockaded round about with the solid trunks of trees, abundant materials for which were found at hand; a broad and deep ditch surrounded the stockade, and the ground in front presented the usual impediment of a thick line of felled trees, the numerous branches of which were sharpened at the point, rendering it both difficult and dangerous to reach the ditch, the garrison within keeping up a destructive and certain fire upon the assailants while they forced their passage through the abatis. Finding himself again thus strongly posted, the Burmese commander next endeavoured to combine treachery within our lines, to force from without; trusting to the strength of his position for safety against any aggressive operations on our part, and prepared, at a moment's warning, to rush in upon us even in the dead of night, as soon as his meditated plans of treachery should take effect.

The population of Rangoon was already considerable, when it received an immense addition by the defeats and subsequent retreat of the Burmese army. Upon the latter occasion, numerous deserters, some of them accompanied by their families, came into the town; all who returned unarmed, whether they had served or not, were freely admitted, and many who had but a few days before been in arms against us, were now living in peace and harmony with our troops. Among this last numerous class, although the generality were good and well-disposed, it was not to be expected that there should not be some miscreants, but too ready to enter into the schemes for our destruction, formed by their late crafty leader, who not only contrived to open a communication with them, but reinforced their numbers with many bold and desperate characters from his own followers.

Our situation became critical in the extreme: spies, assassins, and incendiaries, lurked in every corner of Rangoon; every native within our lines became an object of suspicion, and the utmost vigilance of the troops, combined -with the energy and decision of their commander, could alone have prevented our losing every advantage of our late successes, by the destruction of our stores and magazines, and the consequent impossibility of our following up the blow that had been given; even if greater disasters did not befall us, from the deep-laid treachery and murderous designs of the Burmese general, and his assassin gang. The inflammable materials of which the town was composed, required but a single fire-brand to envelope our cantonments, and everything they contained, in a general conflagration; while the unseen enemy, lurking in the outskirts of the jungle, were held in constant readiness to rush in upon our lines, during the confusion which so dreaded an occurrence could not fail to produce.

To prevent, as much as possible, the discovery of his meditated plans, the Bandoola caused a report to be industriously circulated, of the arrival at his headquarters of a negotiator from Ava, charged with authority to conclude a peace. And so skilfully did his emissaries manage the propagation of this story, that it was very generally believed, that a chief named Mounshoezar, well known as friendly to the British, and from the beginning much against the war, had actually arrived in the neighbourhood of Rangoon, with negotiating powers. But it proved to be, in the sequel, beyond the reach even of this finished dissembler to dupe or lull his watchful antagonist into a moment's inactivity.

Sir Archibald Campbell had no sooner received accurate information of the return, strength, and position of the Burmese army, than he determined to attack them; in the first place to guard against the risk and dangers of delay, with such a force, and so many traitors around us, as well as to prevent the deputy Mounshoezar, should he have arrived, from assuming a lofty tone upon the strength of being supported in his overtures by five-and-twenty thousand men, and to force him to sue for peace in the language of a beaten foe; without which it was but too evident no treaty could be made with so arrogant and false a nation.

Before, however, our arrangements were completed, part of the enemy's plan was carried into effect: at midnight on the 12th of December the long-dreaded cry of fire resounded through the town, and ere an effort could be made to extinguish it, the place was in a blaze. The incendiaries had put the match in several places in those parts of the town most to windward, and, aided by a high wind, the flames flew from house to house, and from street to street, with amazing violence and rapidity, and it seemed beyond the reach of human means to arrest their progress; fortunately our depot of stores and ammunition was in another quarter of the town to that which had been fired, and to save them alone, was now the only thing thought of, or attempted. The drum beat to arms, and the troops on every part of our position were formed in readiness to receive the enemy's expected movement from the jungle; but the promptitude and regularity with which the different corps were drawn up upon their posts most probably arrested the meditated attack—at least none was made, and every disposable man was immediately employed in assisting to extinguish the flames, which now burned with awful splendour, and illumined the whole adjacent country; but by the united exertions of the troops, in the course of two hours they were completely got under control, without any serious damage being sustained in the military property, though not until more than half the town had been destroyed.

After such a specimen of the Bandoola's plans and power of carrying them into effect, and the prospect of his attempting any decided measures being; extremely doubtful, every arrangement was speedily completed for dislodging him from his threatening position, and for driving him to such a distance from our neighbourhood as might enable us to organize, in peace, our means for breaking up from quarters, and for moving forward upon Prome.

In determining to become the assailant, the British commander had again to encounter many: serious difficulties, which required all his experience, knowledge of his enemy, and unbounded confidence in the intrepidity and steadiness of his troops to overcome. He had to guard against the secret movements of an insidious enemy, whose greatly superior numerical strength, correct sources of information, and perfect acquaintance with the jungles, might induce them to make a sudden rush upon Rangoon, during the absence of the corps destined to attack Kokeen. He had to assault, unaided by artillery, or at most by one or two light field-pieces, a formidable fieldwork, defended by at least twenty thousand men; and he had to march out to that position through the narrow and winding footpath of a thick forest, where a well-posted body of native sharp-shooters might thin his ranks long ere he reached the enemy's stronghold: there was, however, no alternative, and the 15th was fixed upon for the reduction of Kokeen.

Early in the morning of that day the corps of attack, in all fifteen hundred men (the rest of the force being left to guard the lines), moved out from their cantonments, and were allowed to march without molestation through the forest to the enemy's position; on reaching which, the little column first became aware of the desperate nature: of the service they had to perform. On debouching from the forest, a field-work presented itself, of such a character as made the veteran soldiers sensible it could be defended, by resolute men, against any disparity of numbers, and the first glance assured them it was held by fearful odds, in the full confidence which its strength inspired. Their minds, however, were firmly wound up to the trial; they viewed the enemy's imposing force with that calm indifference and cool determination which has raised the name of the British soldier so pre-eminently high among the nations of Europe, and had already impressed our present enemy with .due respect and value for their character. They had been too long accustomed to success to doubt its attainment, even on the present occasion; and formidable as the place appeared, they well knew there was no retreating. and that no choice was left between victory and an honourable grave.

The troops had scarcely cleared the forest, when the enemy's sharp-shooters commenced annoying them in flank and rear, and accelerated the necessary disposition for immediate attack; one column, consisting of the Thirteenth Light Infantry, and the Eighteenth Madras Infantry, under Brigadier-General Cotton, was directed to move round the stockade by its left, and assault it in flank, firing a gun, to mark his having reached his point, and being in readiness to move forward; the remainder of the corps, under the commander of the forces, consisting of the Thirty-Eighth, Forty-First, and Eighty-Ninth British regiments, with detachments from the other regiments of Native Infantry, were formed in two columns ready to assault in front. The signal gun was no sooner fired, than the troops with their scaling ladders moved steadily forward; the enemy, apparently regarding the attempt as madness, continued for some time stamping and beating time together, with their hands upon their breasts, and their muskets at the shoulder, instead of attempting to check the assailants while yet at a sufficient distance from their works; and when at length they did open a fire, it proved all too late to save them from defeat; the troops had already reached the ditch, and were in a great measure protected from its effects.

Brigadier-General Cotton's column experienced the greatest difficulty in reaching the interior of the stockade: they bad several strong entrenchments to carry before they gained the main work; in doing which, four officers and a considerable number of men of the Thirteenth Regiment were killed, and many officers and men wounded.

The attack in front, uninterrupted by any outworks, instantly succeeded the leading troops entering by escalade, drove the Burmese from their ramparts at the point of the bayonet, and were speedily followed by their comrades from every corner of the work: the enemy no longer thought of resistance for any other object than the preservation of their lives, and the confused multitude, galled by continued volleys, retired in great disorder, through the few outlets in the rear, where, in crossing the narrow plain that led into the jungle, they were met by the Governor-General's body-guard of cavalry, by whose well-used sabres many perished.

The interior of the stockade, as well as the ditch, were strewed with dead and dying, and many of the enemy, who found escape impossible, with the never-failing cunning and ingenuity of their nation, besmeared themselves with blood, and lay down under the dead bodies of their comrades, in the hope of escaping when darkness set in, but where they were mostly discovered, and made prisoners. Here ended the operations in front of Rangoon: the British troops returned, the same evening, to their cantonments, and the remnant of the Burmese army retreated finally upon Donoobew, leaving posts on the Lain and Panlang rivers, to harass and detain the British force in moving forward.

CHAPTER 12

The Bandoola Retreats

The retreat of Maha Bandoola left the field completely open in our front. Not a man in arms remained in the neighbourhood of Rangoon; and numbers of the people, at length released from military restraint, and convinced of the superiority of the British troops over their countrymen, and of their clemency and kindness to the vanquished, poured daily into Rangoon: even those who had borne arms gave up the cause as hopeless, and returned with their families from a life of suffering and oppression, to the blessings of quiet and undisturbed domestic happiness.

The appearance of the unfortunate people who had passed so many months in the unwholesome jungles, exposed to the inclemencies of an unusually severe monsoon, was truly miserable: they had been kept, even to the women, at constant hard labour in constructing stockades and defences, which were successively taken from them as soon as finished; subjected to the cruelties and ill treatment of innumerable petty chiefs, using, with despotic severity, their arbitrary and brief authority; destitute of the usual necessaries of life, and forced to subsist, in a great measure, upon roots and herbs. Many had perished under the accumulation of misery, or been cut off, for the most trivial offences, by the orders of their merciless despots— most of those who returned to their former dwellings having to lament the loss of a parent, son, or brother.

Familiarized from infancy, however, to occurrences of this nature, our Burmese friends did not long lament such everyday misfortunes, but set zealously to work in building and repairing their houses, and soon began to resume their former trades and avocations.

In the course of a very few days a bazaar made its appearance; at first upon a small scale, but subsequently venison, fish, fruit, and country vegetables could be procured in great abundance. Beef, their religion did not allow them to traffic in; but there was no scarcity of buffaloes for the ample supply of all the troops. But by far the most important result attending the return of the inhabitants to their houses, was the means which they afforded of equipping canoes for the transport of provisions, and of obtaining servants and drivers for the commissariat, with which the force was very scantily provided, owing to the impossibility of inducing that class of people in Bengal, to volunteer their services in Ava.

At first the number of Burmese boats and boatmen was small, and quite inadequate for the conveyance of the requisite supplies, even when the army was only a few marches from Rangoon; but by kind treatment and liberal payment, they subsequently increased so much in numbers, as for some time to meet all the exigencies of the service, until our gradually increasing distance from the depot compelled us to seek for aid from other quarters.

The constant arrival of transports from both presidencies, and the bustle of preparation, produced a happy change in the appearance of Rangoon. Before the end of January, His Majesty's Forty Seventh Regiment; two squadrons of cavalry, horse artillery, and rocket troop; also seventeen hundred cattle, with corresponding equipments, were landed at Rangoon; and His Majesty's Royal regiment, with several battalions of Madras Native Infantry, were under orders for the same service. But even so late in the season as January, had every arrangement been complete, the low Delta, through which we had to march to reach the Irrawaddy, was not sufficiently dry for the passage of artillery, or to insure the troops against disease, from the still wet and unwholesome state of the country.

The 10th day of February was, however, fixed for the commencement of the advance; and although, from the shortness of the season for active operations, we could not hope to reach higher than Prome, the reduction of that important place, with the consequent liberation of Pegu, might lead to pacific negotiations. Even the defence of Donoobew, which had been fortified with all the skill of Burmese art, was considered by many as the last struggle of the court of Ava; and when the formidable preparations of the Indian government, in other quarters, are considered, there was certainly strong reason for anticipating an early termination of the contest.

On the south-east frontier of Bengal, for the invasion of Arracan, a large and well-appointed force, under Brigadier-General Morrison, only awaited the proper season for advancing through the insalubrious jungles of Arracan; and after the reduction of the capital of that province, it was thought not improbable that the Brigadier-General might be enabled to cross the lofty range of mountains (Anoupectoumiew) which separate Arracan from Ava, by one of the little-known and difficult passes, and join Sir Archibald Campbell on the Irrawaddy.

On the Sylhet frontier, another large force, under Brigadier-General Shouldham, threatened to advance through Cassay upon the enemy's capital; and in Assam, Lieutenant-Colonel Richards, with a small field corps, was prepared to drive the enemy from his conquests in that quarter.

The means of the British commander at Rangoon did not enable him to equip a large land column, nor under any circumstances would it probably have been practicable to attempt an exclusive land movement, upon a point at the distance of six hundred miles from his depots; an unlimited command of carriage could alone have enabled him to do so—in which case he might, probably have advanced by the shortest and best road upon the capital, *via* Pegu and Tonghoo, turning all the enemy's positions on the Irrawaddy, and taking him unprepared on a new line of operations, with his troops posted at a distance. It was, however, obvious, that these advantages must be sacrificed to the one great and important point of securing the river communication, for the conveyance of supplies to the army in the field, and for which purpose a combined land and water movement was determined on—the land column advancing in a direction parallel to, and at no great distance from the river, with a view to mutual co-operation and support; and this decision being made, the Siamese General, though not with any very sanguine hopes of success, was requested to advance with his force upon Tonghoo.

No movement in advance had as yet been made by our cautious and wary allies; probably still impressed with the belief, that ultimately the British troops would have to retire, worn out and disgusted with the sanguinary and inconclusive struggle. It was necessary, however, to keep up appearances; and in answer to the various messages that had been sent, urging them to act, the Siamese chiefs at length sent a complimentary embassy to Martaban, begging to be forwarded to the British headquarters, for the ostensible object of congratulating the British general on his victories over the Burmese, on the part of the court of Bangkok, but probably with the real view of observing the actual state of affairs in Ava. The congratulatory epistle brought by these worthies from the Siamese chiefs, contained many high-flown compliments and professions of friendship, but nothing from which an expectation could be formed of any assistance being derived from that quarter; and the banks of the Irrawaddy thus became the exclusive line of operations from the south. The force equipped for this service fell much below the most moderate calculation of our means.

The land column, under the immediate command of Sir

Archibald Campbell, could not, for want of transport, be in any way increased beyond thirteen hundred European infantry, a thousand Sepoys, two squadrons of dragoons, a troop of horse artillery and a rocket troop; and even for this small force our carriage only sufficed for the conveyance of from twelve to fifteen days' provisions, and then only by the sacrifice of every comfort which men and officers usually enjoy, and to a certain extent, in such a climate, positively require, This column was to move in a direction parallel to the Lain river, driving the enemy from all his posts, upon that branch; and to join the Irrawaddy at the nearest accessible point, for the purpose of co-operating with the marine column proceeding· up the Panlang channel, in driving the Bandoola from Donoobew, should its aid for that purpose be required; and to keep up their supplies, a fleet of commissariat canoes, under an officer of the navy, was to accompany the column as high up the Lain river as the depth: of water would permit.

The point upon which the column would join the Irrawaddy, in a country so little known, could not be fixed. The island formed by the Lain and Panlang rivers, was represented as a wilderness of impassable jungle, but across which it was said the Carians, by Bandoola's order, had cut a path, for the sake of communication from Meondaga on the Lain river, to the Irrawaddy opposite to Donoobew, by which, should it prove correct, it was intended the column should advance; but by much the most certain route, and in many respects the most eligible, led to Sarrawah, an the great river about sixty miles above Donoobew.

The marine column, which was placed under the orders of Brigadier-General Cotton, consisted of eight hundred European Infantry, a small battalion of Sepoys, and a powerful train of artillery: these were embarked in the flotilla consisting of sixty boats, some carrying two, and all of them one piece of artillery twelve and twenty-four pound carronades, and commanded by Captain Alexander of His Majesty's navy escorted by the boats of the men-of-war lying at Rangoon, containing upwards of one hundred British seamen. This force was directed to pass up the Panlang river to the Irrawaddy, and driving the enemy from his stockades at Panlang, to push on with all possible expedition to Donoobew. Another force (the naval part under Captain Marryat, R.N., in His Majesty's sloop *Larne*,) and the troops consisting of the Thirteenth British regiment and the Twelfth Madras Native Infantry, commanded by Major Sale, was embarked in transports for Bassein; after reducing which, it was expected sufficient land carriage might be obtained in the district, to enable them to push on to Donoobew, and form a junction with the water column, or to Hewzedah, where they would open a communication with the land division, and both places were believed to be within fifty miles of Bassein.

The impossibility, however, of procuring sufficient carriage prevented the second part of the instructions from being carried into effect, but the reduction of a place of such importance as Bassein, could not but operate materially in the general result of the campaign. These arrangements completed, on the 11th of February the land column marched from Rangoon to Mienza, eight miles, where they encamped, with the exception of His Majesty's Forty-First regiment, which moved up water as far as Meondaga, for the purpose of affording protection to the provision vessels proceeding up the Lain river, and of clearing its banks from any parties of the enemy which might offer to impede its navigation.

CHAPTER 13

From Rangoon to Donoobew

February 13th 1825. Headquarters joined the camp at Mienza, the road passing through a continued jungle interspersed with numerous and very extensive pine-gardens. Passing our post at Kemmendine, we reached the enemy's strongholds in the forest, where they had so long found refuge during the inclement season. Miles and miles of formidable stockading showed that they were at one time resolved to check our progress at an early stage; while numerous tracks of elephants, and other marks of a Burmhan bivouac, sufficiently denoted that they, at least, did not want numbers to dispute our passage.

On reaching camp, the scene which presented itself was at once grotesque and novel; no double-poled tent bespoke the army of Bengal, or rows of well-pitched rowties that of the sister-presidency; no oriental luxury was here displayed, or even any of the comforts of an European camp, to console the traveller after his hot and weary march; but officers of all ranks couching under a blanket, or Lilliputian tent, to shelter themselves from a meridian sun, with a miserable, half-starved cow or pony, the sole beast of burden of the inmate, tied or picketed in rear, conveying to the mind more the idea of a gipsy bivouac, than of a military encampment. Nothing of the pomp or circumstance of war was here apparent, nor would even the experienced eye have recognised in the little group that appeared but as a speck on the surface of an extensive plain, a force about to undertake the subjugation of an empire, and to fight its way for six hundred miles against climate, privations, and a numerous enemy.

February 14th. At five in the morning the drum beat to arms, and the tawdry camp speedily disappearing, a gallant line alone remained, animated by the finest feeling, and prepared to encounter every difficulty· which might present itself. Our road lay through the jungle, occasionally crossing patches of rice ground, but destitute of both houses and inhabitants. The few Carian villages of the district had been destroyed, and the villagers, oppressed and cruelly treated by the Burmhan chiefs, had either fled or been driven away previous to our advance; no vestige of their dwellings now remained. The wild hog and tiger had alone escaped the general persecution, and now retained undisputed occupation of the woods and once-fertile plains. Encamped on the plain of Mhingladoon—distance eight miles. The plain is extensive, having an old tank in the centre of it, the water of which is both muddy and unwholesome.

February 15th. Marched at daylight, the road running through an extensive plain of rice grounds, and, generally speaking, a mere footpath, requiring much labour to make it passable for guns and wagons. We saw the remains of Carian villages, but not one inhabitant; which was so far accounted for, by the certain information we had received of a body: of the enemy being stationed at Mophee, under Maha Silwah, and occupying an old fort at that place. The march this day did not exceed five miles, owing to the weak state of the commissariat cattle, which long continued to retard our progress.

February 16th. Marched to Carianghoon, distance four miles, and found the village inhabited by the Carian tribe. The houses of these strange people are of the most miserable description—mere pigeon houses perched in the air on poles, with a notched stick, as the sole means of egress and ingress to the dwelling; they are, however·, well adapted for protecting their inmates from the ravages of the periodical deluge, and the still more destructive inroads of prowling tigers, in which the woods abound.

The Carians, although the quietest, and most harmless people in the world, are nevertheless of the strongest and most robust frame: the cultivation of the land in Pegu and the lower provinces, is, in a great measure, left to them; and although their numbers are very limited, such is the fertility of the soil, that they not only keep up the consumption of their own districts, but annually send large quantities of grain to the royal granaries, for the use of the less-fertile provinces of upper Ava. They pay heavy taxes to government, but are free from the conscription laws, and are never called upon for military service. The women generally bear the marks of premature old age, probably from a too liberal share of the hard work falling to them, which, in more civilized countries, devolves wholly upon the male inhabitants.

These people appeared heartily glad to see us, and cheerfully assisted in repairing· the roads; they also brought ducks, fowls, and other articles for sale, for which they found a ready and most profitable market. They willingly undertook to carry letters and communications from one corps of the army to another; and no instance occurred of their having deceived or disappointed their employers. They seemed most anxious for the expulsion of Maha Silwah, from Mophee, (only five miles distant,) and gave much useful information regarding his strength and situation.

February 17th. The column marched in order of attack upon Mophee, and arrived in front of the old fort about eight o'clock in the morning: the advance guard immediately pushed forward to the work, and the enemy was seen rushing into the jungle in the greatest dismay and confusion. Our approach seemed to have been wholly unknown and unexpected; we: found their dinners cooking, and everything bore the appearance of a hasty flight. It certainly reflected no small honour on the good faith of our Carian friends, that our movements, known to so many, should have been so inviolably kept secret. An effort was made to come up with the fugitives, but without success.

February 18th. Halted at Mophee. Sending on a strong advance guard to Meondaga, to endeavour to communicate with Lieutenant-Colonel Godwin's detachment coming up the Lain river. The fort of Mophee is of Talien origin, and coeval with Pegu; its site is well chosen and commanding, and, even in its present state, a few weeks' labour might make it very defensible. Inside we found the splendid mansion of Maha Bandoola, built for him when coming down to Rangoon in all the pomp of state, and with unbounded confidence of speedily returning with many a captive stranger in his train. It had not been inhabited since the Bandoola left it. Maha Silwah, also a man of high rank, had a house built for his own reception near it—it being death for a Burmese to inhabit a house of a higher order of architecture than he is entitled to, and degrading to live in one beneath his rank; it consequently happens, that great chiefs, in travelling, have usually a house built for them at every stage, the poor villagers generally receiving very brief notice of the great man's approach; and woe be to them and to their village, if the house is not completed when he arrives, or one bamboo of the particular order of architecture forgotten.

February 19th. Marched to Meondaga, distance eight miles and a half, the road tolerably good, but for the most part running through a thick jungle. We saw several Carian villages on this day's march, but the poor people had all fled on Bandoola's late advance. We could distinctly trace the several encampments of his army; his troops had overrun the country like swarms of blighting locusts, leaving it waste and desolate wherever they had been.

Meondaga had been an extensive village, on the banks of a rivulet falling into the Lain river, about a mile distant. A piquet of Cassay horse was here stationed, which fled at our approach. Accounts now poured in from all quarters of the Bandoola's having retreated from Donoobew; no certain information could be obtained of any road across the Lain island—on the contrary, the Carian's distinctly stated, that none existed. To Sarrawah, the road was known and certain, with the additional advantage of being able to take on the provision boats many miles farther. The latter route was accordingly fixed on, not only as the best in every point of view, but as the speediest way of reaching Donoobew, should the reports of its evacuation prove incorrect, and the assistance of the column be required there.

February 20th. Marched seven miles and a half, to Beanlaboyah, and encamped on the banks of a dry rivulet, where, by digging a few inches, most, excellent water was obtained. A strong advanced guard was pushed on to Lain, our frail conveyances and jaded cattle being unable to proceed farther, and requiring the shortest marches and greatest care to prevent their becoming totally unserviceable.

February 21st. Marched to Keyzagain, eight miles and a half: the village in ruins, and quite deserted. Here we found some wretched families of Rangoon, wandering through the woods in the greatest misery and want; they gladly accepted the offer of a safe conveyance home by the provision boats, being afraid to attempt the journey by themselves, lest they should again fall into the hands of some of the military parties which still infested the country.

February 22nd. Marched six miles to Lain, and joined the advance guard. Sameness, to a great degree, prevails throughout the Delta as high as Lain: a thick, high, brush-wood jungle, with alternate patches of rice-ground, are the principal features of the district; there are few high trees to give any grandeur to the landscape, and many of the richest plains are lying a barren waste, or bearing a luxuriant crop of noxious weeds, and coarse, rank grass. The country bears no trace of an extensive population; the Carian tribes are thinly scattered about; and even in a time of profound peace, the route we followed must have been lone and dreary: not even a head of game was met with to break the disagreeable monotony of our journey.

February 23rd. Halted. Lain is prettily situated on the banks of the river of that name: we found it quite deserted, but the town uninjured. It is the principal town of an extensive district, and furnishes one thousand fighting men for the service: of the state; but owing to some misunderstanding between the Meuthogee, or head local authority, and Bandoola, had withheld its quota on the late advance of that chief. It is also a war-boat station, and from its central position, communicating by many channels with the Irrawaddy, it is well situated for an establishment of that kind.

From Rangoon to Lain no cows or oxen are to be met with; but the country is abundantly stocked with buffaloes, and we found no difficulty in keeping up a supply of slaughter-cattle of that description. These animals were also tried for draft and carriage, but found incapable of travelling with an army, being exceedingly slow-paced, and constantly requiring water. They may serve well enough for the purposes of agriculture, dragging a heavy load for a short distance from the field to the farm, but can never suit for carriage-cattle to an army; they sink down under the heat of the sun on the shortest march, and choke beyond the power of anything, but water, to save them. The Pegu wagons too, of which a few were procured at Rangoon, although apparently strong and well-built, are not calculated for service; they are heavier than those of Bengal, and break down at the first bad rut.

February 24th. The European part of-the column marched this day to Paulkoon, six miles; the-two Native battalions remaining at Lain to replenish our empty carts from the boats, which reached the town in the course of the day.

February 25th. Marched to Outcan, four miles and a half. During the last two marches, we had skirted the great teak forest of Sarrawaddy, and were shaded from the scorching rays of the sun by a continued canopy of the noblest trees: at intervals the forest opened into rich and fertile plains; and here and there a ruined cottage showed where the lonely woodman or industrious Carian once had lived.

Outcan is a long, straggling village, inhabited by both Burmese and Carians; the former had gone to the woods on hearing of our approach, but the latter were found in their houses, and readily sold their poultry and eggs to no small advantage. These people seem perfectly to understand the value of money, and were by no means scrupulous in charging handsomely for whatever they exposed for sale; probably they received a hint from some followers of the camp, of our national prodigality. Both Burmese and Carians seem remarkably fond of ardent spirits, and, generally speaking, will do more for a glass of brandy than for a sum of money.

February 26th. Marched fourteen miles to Soomza; the road running through a magnificent forest, most of the trees of which, in point of size and straightness, would have made a mainmast for the largest ship in the British navy.

The Burmese governor and his people had retired from Soomza the day previous to our arrival, having first gone through the saving ceremony of firing a volley or two, to encourage a belief that they had fought their ground with us; even that, however, did not save the chief from the vengeance of his superiors. During our stay at Soomza, he became apprehensive of punishment for not having done his duty, and sent in several messages, expressing his anxiety to come in and put himself under our protection; but watched by numerous spies, and wandering about, in constant terror of his life, he could find no opportunity to elude the vigilance of his guards. One of these vile assassins at last came up to the unhappy man with a pretended letter of forgiveness from the Prince of Sarrawaddy; and while his victim was in the act of reading it, with one blow severed his head from his body. At Soomza we found, for the first time, a small herd of cows.

February 27th and 28th. Halted at Soomza to give the two Native battalions time to overtake us. Some prisoners taken here, informed us that the late army of Maha Silwah had entirely dispersed; the men of the lower provinces retiring quietly to their homes, while those from Upper Ava assembled into marauding bands, plundering and burning the defenceless villages as they passed along, and practising the most wanton cruelties among the unfortunate villagers whom chance threw in their way. Parties of the incendiaries were constantly seen at the work of destruction around us, but we found them as expert and clever in escaping punishment, as they were bold and merciless in their savage pursuits.

March 1st. Marched for Theeboon, at one in the morning; twelve miles. Whoever has made a night march, can form some idea of our situation when at length the setting moon left us entering a dark and gloomy forest, through whose verdant canopy no sunbeam ever penetrated; the column, at times, abruptly stopped by natural barriers of thorn and brush-wood, and winding along a narrow and unseen path, holding man to man, to prevent diverging from the track which even our guide could with difficulty follow: all these annoyances, however, are light, when compared with the real evil of a long march by day, exposed to the overpowering heat of a tropical sun. At Theeboon we forded the Lain river, about two feet and a half deep, and took up a position one mile in advance. To this point, the indefatigable perseverance of the naval officer in charge had brought our provision boats, and here all our commissariat carts, and means of transport, were, for the last time, fully replenished. Here a note from Brigadier-General Cotton announced the capture of Panlang, and the immediate advance of the marine column into the Irrawaddy.

March 2nd. Marched to Sarrawah, sixteen miles; and saw, for the first time, the majestic Irrawaddy rolling on, in a deep and rapid stream, towards the ocean, even now, in its lowest state, from seven to eight hundred yards in breadth. Sarrawah is a large and populous town, and is the headquarters of his Burmhan Majesty's war-boats in Pegu. On the march this day, we passed a very extensive tank, absolutely alive from the quantities of fish in it: it is a perquisite of the war-boat establishment, and rents for ten thousand tickalls* a year. On reaching Sarrawah, we had the mortification to find that the whole population of the place, men, women, and children, had already crossed the river, and were now seen on the opposite shore, gazing anxiously at their deserted homes. But, with the exception of two small canoes, all means of communicating with them had been removed: every endeavour, however, through the medium of one or two old priests who remained behind, was ·made to induce them to return; but from fear, or the presence of their chiefs, our invitations proved of no avail: they at length turned their backs upon the river, and were seen, for some time, moving slowly towards an extensive forest, at a short distance from the river, in the deep shades of which they gradually disappeared.

March 3rd, 4th, 5th, and 6th. Halted these four days at Sarrawah, for positive information of the movements of the marine column, during which time not a shot was heard, and accounts continued to pour in from all quarters of Bandoola's retreat from Donoobew. Some said he had gone to Lamina, in the direction of Bassein; others, that he had fled to the mountains of Arracan; but all agreed that he either had retired, or only waited the approach of our troops, that he might be able to do so with some appearance of honour. The distance

---

*About a thousand pounds.

of Sarrawah from Donoobew, in a direct line, may be thirty miles: we were aware that the flotilla must have reached the latter place some days previous to our arrival at the former, and not hearing a shot fired, we naturally concluded the information of the natives would prove correct.

The position of the land column at Sarrawah was highly favourable for cutting off the enemy's retreat by water, and also for preventing them from rallying higher up the river. The only means of crossing the division, to the right bank of the Irrawaddy, consisted in half-a-dozen miserable canoes, which had been collected from the adjacent villages, and as the passage, under such circumstances, could not be effected in less than a week, it was resolved that we should halt a day or two, in expectation of more certain information relative to the real state of affairs at Donoobew.

The occupation of Prome was the grand object of the campaign, a point that the land column alone might have gained, perhaps, with trifling loss, had not its future subsistence been dependant on the flotilla and the free and open navigation of the Irrawaddy. On the other hand, every day's consumption bore heavy on our present slender stores, and increased the anxiety to advance, while they yet sufficed to carry us to Prome; and, once established there, it was presumed the troops might be for some time provisioned from the country, represented as abounding in cattle, and productive in rice.

Too much credit cannot be given to Bandoola and his chiefs, for the secrecy they maintained and enforced, relative to their plans, arrangements, and movements at the present juncture. The state of espionage and terror under which the peasantry are kept, renders them extremely circumspect both in words and actions, and we had here an excellent opportunity of observing its influence supersede all other considerations.

March 7th. Early on the morning of the 7th, the agreeable sound of a heavy cannonade at Donoobew was at last distinctly heard, and received as authentic information from our marine division, which was now beyond a doubt in the act of attacking the place. The cannonade lasted till near two o'clock, p.m., when it entirely ceased, and left a strong conviction on our minds that Donoobew had fallen—numerous natives, in the course of that day and the following night, confirming the belief, by unqualified accounts of Bandoola's total rout. Many urgent reasons called for our immediate advance, as well to prevent the enemy from reaching, and perhaps occupying Prome with his defeated army, as to deprive the people in our front of sufficient time for burning, driving, and laying waste the country, which they would no doubt immediately commence, when the fall of Donoobew was known. The following day was, however, given to the chance of hearing from Brigadier-General Cotton, and accounts still poured in of the Bandoola's hasty retreat.

March 9th. On this day the division advanced inland to near Segaybeen, leaving a strong detachment at Sarrawah, to prevent any part of the enemy's troops from retreating by water, and to communicate with the marine column, as well as to urge all possible exertion in forwarding supplies to Prome. The road on this day's march lay mostly through a jungle, and the open patches we occasionally met with bore no appearance of recent cultivation; the few villages we found in ruins, and the country wholly deserted by its: inhabitants. Distance, twelve miles.

March 10th. Marched to U-au-deet, distance fourteen miles. On this march we again crossed the Lain river, (about two feet deep,) near the village of Nangur, and about eight miles from where it leaves the Irrawaddy. During the rains this branch is navigable for vessels of considerable burthen, and cutting off a large angle of the distance is sometimes preferred as the most eligible route to Prome. U-au-deet is a town of considerable extent, upon the banks of the great river: we found it wholly deserted, and every article that could be of use to us carried away. No mark of hurry or confusion remained, to warrant a belief that a terrified people had fled in dismay, to avoid falling into the hands of an enemy: on the contrary, the desertion of the towns and villages was obviously a systematical arrangement of the Burmhan chiefs; and showed how necessary and desirable a rapid march would be, to save our promised winter-quarters from a similar fate. Here we heard, for the first time, that the King had ordered a house to be built for himself at Prome; and had given out, that if the English continued their audacious march upon his capital, there he would in person meet them, and give them signal cause to repent such rash and bold proceedings.

March 11th. Early in the morning official intelligence was received, that our troops had failed in their attack upon the outworks of Donoobew, and that, without a large reinforcement, the place could not be carried, being both strong and well defended by a numerous garrison. On receiving this unpleasant and unexpected news, two questions naturally arose,—whether to push on to Prome with the land column, and reinforce Brigadier-General Cotton from the rear, by a strong detachment which was about to move forward from Rangoon, under Brigadier Mac-Creagh, or at once to retrograde, and finish the business at Donoobew. The latter measure was decided on—the flotilla, upon which the land column depended for supplies, being stopped, and the navigation of the Irrawaddy so completely commanded, that not a canoe could pass the enemy's position. Our commissariat too, at the time, had not ten days' rations left—no reliance could be placed upon the country for furnishing even one day's consumption; the people everywhere fled before us, and even when chance threw an individual in our way, he only answered all our questions and requests, by pointing towards Donoobew, and exclaiming *"Bandoola! Bandoola!"* In a word, starvation stared us in the face at every step had we proceeded; and the occupation· of Prome, however desirable, was not to be attempted under circumstances so eminently hazardous. On the other hand, it became every day more certain that the Bandoola's army was the chief, if not the only force now left to oppose us; and the nation evidently looked. to them alone for checking our advance, These circumstances had been most carefully concealed, and every native rumour and report, up to the time of our hearing the cannonade already mentioned, tended to confirm us in the belief that Bandoola had neither means nor inclination to defend his post against a spirited attack.

March 12th. Early in the morning the column returned to Thariandoon, which we had passed on the march two days before.

March 13th. The column again reached Sarrawah; and here an obstacle of a most serious nature presented itself. To reach Donoobew, the Irrawaddy, one of the widest and most rapid rivers of the East, must, be crossed by an army, with cavalry, artillery, and commissariat equipment, and unprovided with any means for such an undertaking, beyond a few small canoes, which had been with difficulty, procured. Energy and perseverance, however, aided by the cheerful and hearty exertions of the soldiers, finally triumphed over every obstacle. In the course of this day, the infantry of the Madras division were rapidly crossed, and pushed on to Henzedah, to occupy a position in advance.

March 14th. Rafts were constructed to cross the artillery, stores, and commissariat; and by continued labour, day and night, on the fifth day every man had reached in safety the right bank of the Irrawaddy.

March 18th. Headquarters were established at Henzedah. Here a report was received from the commanding officer at Bassein, intimating his intention of endeavouring to form a junction, by going up to Lamina, situated about twenty miles up the Bassein river, in boats; where, if any carriage was. procurable, he would push on to Henzedah. Intimation, at the same time, being received, that the Kee Wongee* was posted on the road leading from Lamina, about fifteen miles distant, with a small but daily increasing force, Lieutenant-Colonel Godwin, with a strong detachment, marched,, soon after night closed, to endeavour to surprise the Wongee with an unexpected visit. The vigilance of the enemy was not to be eluded; beacon after beacon, gleaming through the darkness of the night, warned the watchful sentinels of the sleeping minister, that danger was at hand, and the astonished Wongee lost no time in preparing for inglorious flight. Regardless of his honour, and indifferent to the fate of his followers, the unwarlike premier thought only of his own safety—neither attempting to maintain order among his people, nor availing himself of their local knowledge, which might have ensured a safe retreat; but feeling his warlike robes sit irksome on his shoulders, he wisely threw them off, and fled almost unattended, in the simple and saving garb of a peasant. The obedient levies willingly followed the example of their chief, and fled into the jungle. Two Saradogees (secretaries) of the Lotoo, probably not much skilled in riding, and more accustomed to use the pen than the sword, were the only dead left upon the field.

March 19th and 20th. During the two following days, the division was halted, while the commissariat, &c. &c. were preparing and re-loading their carts. Henzedah, and Keoum-zeik adjoining, form a considerable town, of at least two miles in length, but very narrow. The river, running under a high bank, is deep and rapid.

We found the place wholly deserted, except by packs of meagre dogs, who kept up an incessant howling for their absent masters, although, in this country, they seem, like cats, more susceptible of local than of personal attachment, and are rarely induced to leave the houses they have been

*Principal minister of the Lotoo, or council of state.

brought up and fed in. Numerous pagodas and religious buildings alone distinguish Henzedah and Keoum-zeik from the meanest villages; and, generally speaking, the remark holds good through the whole of Ava: the houses are much alike, and mostly built of the same materials; those of the chiefs and priests are alone distinguished by the number of roofs, one above another, and the other architectural insignia of their respective dignities and rank.

Henzedah enjoyed considerable advantages as a commercial place, and had been in a flourishing state previous to our arrival. It was inhabited by some Armenians, and other merchants, who cultivated indigo, which, in this country, thrives remarkably well, without the crops being to the risk and uncertainty, which, in Bengal, is often productive of much mischief; and carried on an extensive traffic between Lamina, Rangoon; and the upper country. The plains were covered with cattle, but whatever use the natives may have made of them, to us they were wilder than the mountain deer, and our daily consumption was barely kept up from the numerous herds, by the utmost exertion of the commissariat.

March 21st. The army marched to Legzey—thirteen miles and a half; chiefly jungle, and the few houses we met with deserted.

March 22nd. Marched twelve miles, through a heavy grass jungle, to Yeong-ben-zay. Here we were obliged to remain halted while the pioneers cut a road through a grass and reed jungle, in general ten, in some places, twenty feet high; with incredible labour, that invaluable corps succeeded in cutting a good path a distance of nearly ten miles; and on the 24th, the column again advanced twelve miles, halting at a village, from which we had a tolerable view of the enemy's works, distant only four miles. A fleet of war-boats lay above the stockade, at a little island; and on the approach of a reconnoitring party from our camp, they came out in very pretty style, and commenced a cannonade. The flotilla was also seen lying at anchor some distance below the stockade, and everything seemed to promise a speedy trial of strength with the now confident and emboldened garrison. The place was described as being very strong, well provided with artillery, and filled with the enemy's best soldiers, commanded by their favourite general; and although the fine season was drawing near its close, the preservation of lives was the first consideration of our commander, who was resolved to take every advantage science might afford in the reduction of the place, instead, as we expected, of attempting to carry it by a *coup de main*.

March 25th. The army moved upon Donoobew, and endeavoured to invest the fort, at long gun-shot distance: it was, however, found much too extensive to admit of its being surrounded even by a chain of posts, by so small a force; and a position was consequently taken up—our left resting on the river above the stockade, and the right extending in a circular direction towards the centre of the rear face of the fort. While this was going forward, the enemy manned his works, and fired upon us from a great many guns; numerous golden *chattahs* glittered in the morning sun, with an effect that would have been imposing to any one but those who had so often seen these proud emblems of command vanish before the powerful magic of a well-pointed volley, or a gallant charge; when the boldest chiefs were glad to shun the dangerous token of imperial favour, and even the humble bearers to throw from them the honourable badge upon which every musket seemed to bear. The enemy's cavalry hovered on our flanks while we continued in motion; and everything about the stockade bespoke system and judgment in the chief, with order, confidence, and regularity in the garrison.

CHAPTER 16

Fighting at Donoobew

The stockade of Donoobew extended for nearly a mile along a sloping bank of the Irrawaddy—its breadth varying according to the nature of the ground, from five to eight hundred yards.: The stockading was composed of solid teak beams, from fifteen to seventeen feet high, driven firmly into the earth, and placed as closely as Possible to each other; behind this wooden wall the old brick ramparts of the place rose to a considerable height, strengthening the front defences by means of crossbeams, and affording a firm and elevated footing to the defendants. Upwards of a hundred and fifty guns and swivels were mounted on the works, and the garrison was protected from the shells of the besiegers by numerous well-contrived traverses and excavations.

Bandoola's force at this time did not probably exceed fifteen thousand men, but it was chiefly composed of the veterans who had accompanied him from Arracan, and, generally speaking, men of more tact and military knowledge than the raw levies, which had been raised upon the spur of the occasion. A ditch of considerable magnitude and depth surrounded the defences, the passage of which was rendered still more difficult by spikes, nails, holes, and other contrivances. Beyond the ditch several rows of strong railing were next interposed; and in front of all, an abatis, thirty yards broad, and otherwise of a most formidable description, extended round the place, except on the river face, where the deep and rapid Irrawaddy presented a sufficient barrier—its breadth at this season not exceeding seven hundred yards; and not a boat could pass without being exposed to a heavy fire from the stockade.

Before the right face, or that lowest down the river, two strong outworks were constructed, the first-of which had been taken by the marine column, the second having· proved too strong to be carried by so small a force. A heavy and extensive jungle intervened between the right and rear faces, covering about a third of the latter, beyond which, however, a fine open plain extended to the river; upon this plain, at long-shot distance from the fort, the: division was encamped, and preparations immediately commenced for breaking ground and proceeding systematically against the place.

The camp being pitched, the enemy at once desisted from further annoyance, and the heavy fire which he had kept up all morning entirely ceased; but there was a something in the calm, in the sudden disappearance of the defendants from their ramparts, the occasional patrolling of small parties of horse, and the long-continued observation of our line by a party of chiefs, from an elevated watch-tower, that foreboded a very early interruption to the present stillness of the scene. Even the careless soldiers seemed to regard the momentary repose as seamen do a treacherous lull between the violent gusts of the increasing storm; and each sentinel, when the night had closed, stood prepared upon his post for the sudden appearance of an enemy—listening anxiously for some sound which might indicate where the conflict would begin: nor were they long kept in suspense or doubt. The clock had struck ten, and the moon was fast approaching to the verge of the horizon, when sharp musketry, and the loud war-cry of the enemy, roused the sleeping camp. The wearied soldiers, starting from a profound repose, mechanically seized -their muskets, which every man had carefully placed by his side, and were quickly drawn up in readiness to receive the noisy visitors, who had so unkindly robbed them of their rest.

The line was scarcely formed when the enemy's intention became apparent: his columns were distinctly heard moving in an oblique direction towards our right, for the purpose of turning it; at the same time keeping up a distant fire upon the left and centre, to encourage a belief that these were the selected points. On reaching and outflanking our extreme right, apparently at no great distance, the two regiments on the right of the line rapidly changed front to the right, and kneeling, to insure a better aim, kept up a rapid running fire, which instantly checked the advancing columns; and although they repeated their attempt more than once, every succeeding effort became more feeble, until they at last returned in hopeless silence to their irritated and disappointed commander, who did not fail to give the usual Burmhan reward for failure, to such as had been most conspicuously unsuccessful on the occasion.

The night was very dark, and enabled the enemy to carry off their killed and wounded, which could not be few. On our side, only two or three men were killed, and twenty wounded.

March 26th. No communication having yet been opened with the marine column, a party of one hundred European infantry and a few cavalry were sent early this morning to march round the enemy's works, keeping at a respectful distance, in order to reach the fleet at its station below Donoobew. The road lay partly through a thick jungle, but, with the aid of three elephants, a passage was forced, and the party reached the fleet without firing a shot. After requesting the naval commander to move up, and form a junction, the party endeavoured to return, but found the jungle so strongly occupied by the enemy, that it would have cost many lives to force a passage through them; and as there was no particular object to be gained, they were prudently ordered back, to come up with Brigadier-General Cotton on the following day.

A little above Donoobew, the river forms an island, the channel on either side being about four hundred yards broad.

In the farther channel lay the enemy's war-boats, fifteen in number, from which they occasionally turned their prows round the corner of the island, and fired into our camp.

A party of seventy men, with a few rockets, were, in consequence, crossed over to the island: the boats at first drew up, and appeared inclined to maintain their station, but the unpleasant hissing of a shower of rockets quite disconcerted them; and if they did not show much gallantry on the occasion, they at least gave us a tolerable specimen of their chief merit—that of flying with incredible speed. An old pagoda, about three hundred yards from the enemy's defences, being chosen as the most eligible point for breaking ground, it was accordingly occupied by His Majesty's Forty-Seventh regiment early in the night. The working parties immediately commenced operations, and at daylight a considerable extent of trench was completed. The ground about the pagoda was found mined and loaded, but owing to the inexperience of the miners, it did no harm; indeed, if it had gone off, it would have done no more than scorch the standers by.

March 27th. At nine o'clock this morning, the flotilla was seen in full sail up the river; and they were no sooner observed than the garrison sortied in considerable force, infantry and cavalry, with seventeen war elephants, fully caparisoned, and carrying a proportion of armed men, This attack was, as usual, directed upon our right; and while the flotilla came up in full sail, under all the fire of the fort, the cavalry, covered by the horse artillery, was ordered to charge the advancing monsters: the scene was novel and interesting; and although neither the elephants nor their riders can ever be very formidable in modern warfare, they stood the charge with a steadiness and courage these animals can. be rarely brought to show. Their riders were mostly shot, and no sooner did the elephants feel themselves unrestrained by the hand of their drivers,· than they walked back to the fort with the greatest composure. The flotilla having passed the fort, with trifling loss, anchored on our left During the heavy cannonade that took place between the boats and the stockade, the Bandoola, who was superintending the practice of his artillery, gave his garrison a specimen of the discipline he meant to enforce, in this last struggle to retrieve his lost character and reputation. A Burmese officer being killed while pointing a gun, by a, shot from the flotilla, his comrades, instantly abandoning the dangerous post, could not be brought back to their duty by any remonstrances of their chiefs; when Bandoola, stepping down to the spot, instantly severed the heads of two of the delinquents from their bodies, and ordered them to be stuck up upon the spot *"pour encourager les autres"*.

March 28th. The working parties continued making approaches towards the place; and the steam vessel and some light boats, pushing up the river after the enemy's war-boats, succeeded in capturing nine of them (four gilt): their crews, when likely to be run: down by the steam-boat, jumping into the river, where they are quite in their element, effected their escape.

March 29th, 30th, and 31st. Continued constructing batteries, and landing heavy ordnance; the enemy on their part remaining very quiet, and busily employed in strengthening their works. On the evening of the 31st, a Burmese came out of the fort with a piece of dirty canvass, containing the following laconic epistle from the Bandoola:"In war we find each other's force; the two countries are at war for nothing, and we know not each others minds!!!"The bearer, on being interrogated as to the meaning of such obscure and bravadoing language, as well as to the insulting manner in which the message was delivered, said be was merely a common soldier, and knew nothing of the matter, but believed his chief wished to make peace: on being threatened, however, with punishment as a spy, he at last confessed there had been a grand consultation held in the Bandoola's house; and it was thought in the garrison that his intention was to sally upon us at the head of his whole force, the first favourable opportunity, and to conquer or perish in the attempt.

April 1st. The mortar batteries and rockets began the work of destruction this morning, and continued firing, at intervals, during the day and succeeding night, the enemy remaining under the protection of their works, and making little return to our fire.

April 2nd. At daylight the breaching batteries opened, and almost immediately afterwards two Lascars*, who had been prisoners in the fort, came running out, and informed us, that Bandoola had been killed the day before by a rocket; and that no entreaty of the other chiefs could prevail upon the garrison to remain, the whole having fled or dispersed, during the preceding night the British line was, in consequence, immediately under arms, and the place taken possession of. Sufficient proof remained in the interior, of the hurry and confusion of the flight; not a gun was, removed, and even the large depot of grain which bad been formed, remained uninjured—the dread of detection having prevented the enemy from putting the torch to what they well knew would be a most valuable acquisition to the British army. In the fort we found a number of wounded men, who all concurred in saying their general had been killed; and one poor fellow, with both his feet shot off, related the story so circumstantially, as to leave no doubt whatever of the fact; it was as follows:

I belonged to the household of Menghi Maha Bandoolah, and my business was to beat the great drums that are hanging in the veranda of the Wongee's house. Yesterday morning, between the hours of nine and ten, while the chiefs dinner was preparing, he went out to take his usual morning walk round the works, and ar-

---

*Bengal native seamen.

rived at his observatory, (that tower with a red ball upon it,) where, as there was no firing, he sat down upon a couch that was kept there for his use. While he was giving orders to some of his chiefs, the English began throwing bombs, and one of them falling close to the Wongee, burst, and killed him on the spot: his body was immediately carried away and burned to ashes; his death was soon known to everybody in the stockade, and the soldiers refused to stay and fight under any other commander. The chiefs lost all influence and command over their men, every individual thinking only of providing for his own personal safety.

But, even in a desultory and disorderly ·flight of this nature, the characteristic cunning and caution of the nation was conspicuous,. effecting their retreat with such silence and circumspection, as would have been a lesson to the best disciplined army in Europe.

The character of Maha Bandoola seems to have been a strange mixture of cruelty and generosity, talent with want of judgment, and a strong regard to personal safety, combined with great courage and resolution, which never failed him till death. The acts of barbarous cruelty he committed are-too numerous to be related: stern and inflexible in all his decrees, he appears to have experienced a, savage pleasure in witnessing the execution of his bloody mandates; even his own hand was ever ready to punish with death the slightest mark of want of zeal in those he had entrusted with commands, or the defence of any post. Still his immediate adherents are said to have been sincerely attached to him; uncontrolled license to plunder and extort from all who were unfortunate enough to meet Bandoola's men, may no doubt have reconciled them to their situation, and confirmed them much in their attachment to their leader. The management of a Burmese army, for so long a period contending against every disadvantage to which a general can be subjected, evinced no small degree of talent, while the position and defences at Donoobew, as a field-work, would have done credit to the most scientific engineer; but it is difficult to account for his motives, or give, credit to his judgment, in giving up the narrow rivers of Panlang and Lain, where a most effectual opposition could have been given, to fight his battle on the banks of the broad Irrawaddy, where the ground was favourable to the regular movement of disciplined troops. During the days of his prosperity, Bandoola seldom exposed his person: in the battles of Rangoon and Kokeen, he was never under fire; but he did not hesitate, when circumstances required it, to allow himself to be hemmed in at Donoobew, where he boldly declared he would conquer or die, and till he actually fell, set his men the first example of the courage he required in all.

April 4th. The column re-commenced its march for Prome.

April 12th. On this day, we were again on the left bank of the Irrawaddy at Sarrawah.

April 14th. We reached U-au-deet, from which we had retrograded just one month before, having in that time marched one hundred and sixty miles, twice crossed the Irrawaddy, and finished the war in the lower provinces of Pegu. On our march to U-au-deet, bands of fugitives from Donoobew were occasionally heard of, but they kept at a distance from our line of march, and in no instance attempted any species of annoyance. Heartily tired of a profitless and hopeless contest, personal security seemed the only object of the good; while those whose trade was war, plunder, and rapine, saw, in the distracted state of their government, the best opportunity of indulging their natural propensities, and scoured the country in bands, turning the arms, that were given them to oppose the invaders of their territory, into weapons of destruction against the unprotected peasantry who attempted to resist their arbitrary demands.

April 15th. The column marched to Sabaye-meum, nine miles—separated from the river at this season of the year by an extensive sand-bank. Not an inhabitant was to be seen, the whole country as high as Prome having been cleared of its population as soon as the fate of Donoobew was decided.

April 16th. On this day we marched to Monghee, seven miles, where we found the ground marked out for a very extensive stockade, one face of which was nearly finished; it had been begun by the force under Prince Sarrawaddy, whose encampment we found in the rear, containing huts capable of holding several thousand men. The surrounding country pretty open, and mostly arable land.

April 17th. Moved to Bamah-zeik, on the great river, a very delightful spot, where a Burmese force had also been quartered, and a greater number of houses of the order of nobility were observed than at any encampment we had yet seen.

April 18th. Marched to Sembuen—seven miles.

April 19th. We reached Huddadoon, five miles, where the Anoupectomiew, or Arracan mountains, were first distinctly visible. The landscape here was beautiful indeed; but the still smoking ashes of once happy villages cast a deep shade of sadness over the scene. In the evening a messenger, rather an elderly man, came in from Prome, the bearer of a pacific communication from the chiefs of the Burmhan army; the old man drank much too freely for a diplomatist, and when he rose to take his departure, whispered in the general's ear, "They are frightened out of their senses, and you may do what you please with them."

The subject of the communication was the desire of the King and government of Ava to terminate the war by treaty: the writers represented themselves as two Attawoons, or counsellors of His Majesty, who had been sent down to Prome for that special purpose. An answer was returned expressive of the readiness of the Indian Government to conclude a peace, and that upon the arrival of the British force at Prome, every opportunity and facility in opening negotiations would be afforded.

April 20th. Marched twelve miles, to Tirrup-mew, which we found destroyed.

April 21st. We reached Laing-wah, eight miles. The country over which we marched is very beautiful; the vista on either hand, bounded by a distant chain of mountains, with the magnificent Irrawaddy running through a richly variegated country, completes a landscape seldom surpassed, or even rivalled.

April 22nd and 23rd. Marched to Kongkraing, seven miles and a half; and, on the following day, to within a short distance of Shudaung-mew, formerly the frontier fortress of the kingdom of Pegu.

April 24th. Marched to Daringa-boy-ah, eight miles; from whence the heights of Prome were distinctly seen, with our flotilla lying at anchor a short distance below the town. Here another letter from the Burmese authorities of Prome was received, in answer to that sent to them by the first messenger, couched in very ambiguous, and even insolent, terms. They demanded that the city should not be occupied by the British troops, observing that there were armies on both sides, and that the space between them was sufficiently large to afford a place of meeting; the general tone of the communication induced a strong suspicion that the chiefs were not acting honestly, and it was determined the town should immediately be taken possession of. An answer was accordingly sent back, to say, that the military occupation of Prome could not be dispensed with, but that the English general would be happy to meet the Burmhan deputies at any place and time, next day, they might fix upon, to arrange whatever might be expedient for the protection of the inhabitants and their property.

April 25th. The column, in order of battle, was again in motion, some hours before day, although information had in the interim been received that the Burmhan chiefs, foiled in their treacherous object of gaining time to enable expected reinforcements to arrive, had retreated with all their people in the greatest precipitation· At daylight we found ourselves under the ridge of hills which cover Prome to the southward, stretching a considerable distance to the south-east and east, while the river to the west forms an excellent barrier on that side, commanded from every hill for a distance of at least a mile; each hill was fortified to the very summit, and a more formidable position than that we stood in front of, has seldom been encountered. The stockades, however, were unoccupied: the enemy having evacuated every post, and the column, pushing on to the city, found it already in a blaze; every exertion was immediately made to save it from the flames, which were at length got under control, after destroying a great part of the town. The treacherous views of the Burmhan chiefs were now fully ascertained. The town and position in its front had been fortified with the greatest care; and after the dispersion of the Bandoola's army at Donoobew, all eyes were turned to Prome, as the only point at which the invading army could be stopped; and the utmost energy of the local authorities was employed in organizing such a force as would enable them to prevent the British from establishing themselves in so desirable a situation. New generals were appointed, fresh levies were called out, and a numerous artillery was on its way from Ava, with which to crown the summits of the various hills; in a word, the whole disposable force of the kingdom was concentrating at a spot rendered memorable by the many sanguinary battles that had formerly been fought between them and the Peguers.

The rapid advance of the British force appears to have been wholly unexpected, and to have defeated all their plans. Sir Archibald Campbell was within three days' march of Prome, and not a man of the expected reinforcements had yet reached that place; but they were known to be within a, few days' march of it, and the Burmhan chiefs, forgetting every principle of honour and good faith, did not hesitate, for the purpose of gaining a few days' time, to open a negotiation, in the hope that their object would be gained before their treachery was discovered. Unfortunately for them, sincerity or honesty of dealing have never been rated among their virtues or good qualities; and obscure and equivocal overtures from such a quarter were only regarded as a signal for greater promptitude and decision in the prosecution of our march. To that opinion of our enemy, the fall of Prome may be ascribed; had two days' delay been granted, it would have cost us many lives to carry it by force.

The deputies, finding themselves foiled at their own weapons, at once threw off the mask, and employed the brief space left them in burning and destroying everything they supposed could be of use to us; and, in the utmost confusion, began their disgraceful flight, headed by the Prince of Sarrawaddy, burning and laying waste the villages on their route, driving thousands of helpless, harmless people from their houses to the woods.

CHAPTER 15

Operations Around Prome

The conduct and treacherous designs of the chiefs at Prome had now effectually dispelled the anticipations we had so confidently indulged in, of some decisive result attending the conquest of Pegu. It was evident we had again miscalculated the impression such an event was likely to produce, as well as the means and resources of the enemy, and had yet to learn more fully the proud and obstinate character of the government we had to deal with. Distrust and jealousy of our motives and professions may, no doubt, have had some weight in stimulating His Burmese Majesty to persevere in the contest; but without inquiring further, at present, into the mixed motives of pride and fear which may have regulated his conduct, it was sufficiently evident, that any prospect of peace was still distant and uncertain.

The remnant, of the Burmese army was collected at Melloone, and orders from the Lotoo, or great council, were forthwith issued for the raising and equipping of thirty thousand men, as a reinforcement to the army; but so changed were circumstances with the government, that instead, as in former times, of the imperial mandate being instantly obeyed, and of men from all parts of the country rallying round the national standard at the first summons of their chiefs, in the hope of honour, rewards, and plunder, every recruit was now paid the sum of from a hundred and fifty to two hundred ticalls (about twenty pounds), as a bounty: it was, however, obvious, that neither cost nor sacrifice of any kind would deter the king from prosecuting the war, and meeting the British army once more in the field at the close of the approaching rainy season.

If any disappointment was felt at the protracted nature of the contest, it was, at least, satisfactory, to find that comfortable and healthy winter-quarters, with abundance of supplies, had been provided for the troops; and that the war had now been carried into a country, known to abound in cattle, from which the army could be well equipped for the ensuing campaign.

A short period of the dry season still remaining, it was not suffered to pass unprofitably: a small corps of observation being lightly equipped for the purpose of clearing the inland districts of Prome of the military bands which overran the country, plundering and oppressing the inhabitants, and driving them, by whole villages, with their cattle and effects, to a distance from the vicinity of the British troops. It was also intended that this corps should move, as far as possible, in the direction of Tonghoo, a walled city, and one of the most important places in the empire, and of which very little is yet known, from its never having been visited by Europeans; at a distance of a hundred miles to the eastward of Prome, and separated from that province by the Galadzet mountains.

The first two days' march to the eastward of Prome was over a rich and fertile country, abounding in extensive plains of rice-grounds from which an abundant harvest had lately been reaped, and a large proportion of the produce, no doubt, been conveyed to Prome, to supply the granaries at that place and other military posts.

As the column advanced farther into the interior, these marks of industry and population rapidly diminished, the country fast assuming the common feature of a luxuriant wilderness, overgrown with lofty forests, rank reeds, and high brushwood jungle, with a few miserable hamlets scattered about at a distance from each other, bearing a striking contrast to the populous and cultivated banks of the Irrawaddy;

and affording a strong reason for believing that the population of Ava has been greatly overrated by our travellers, whose calculations were, probably, either formed from the appearance of the thickly-peopled banks of the river, the only part of the country they had an opportunity of seeing, or drawn from natives, who, from ignorance, or a desire to magnify the greatness of their nation, never fail to estimate their numbers far beyond the truth.

To guard against the panic and alarm, which the appearance of a foreign enemy in these inland districts could not fail to produce, great care was taken to apprize the villages of the approach and friendly intentions of the party; and the inhabitants were, almost in every instance, found occupying their houses, staring in wild amazement at a sight so strange and novel, as the garb and appearance of British soldiers must have presented to them: a very brief acquaintance, however, suffices to inspire confidence, and even familiarity, among this frank and cheerful people, who, as soon as the tents were pitched, might be seen in groups, bartering or selling their fowls, and other articles, to the best advantage, or gladly accepting a glass of brandy from the officers, as they surveyed, with interest and attention, the scene around them.

In many villages, looms were found at work, weaving the coarse striped stuff worn by the natives; and although no symptoms of luxury, or even comfort, could be traced in their abodes, habit had reconciled them to their fate; and neither the cruelty and extortions of their government, nor the state of their country, overrun by foreign troops, and suffering from the barbarous excesses of their own lawless levies, had been able to banish contentment from their homes, or overcome the stoical indifference of this light-hearted and ill-governed race.

Wherever a Burmese force had preceded the British column, desolation marked its track; the wretched villagers, plundered and driven from their abodes, had sought refuge in the forest; and occasionally on its skirts a solitary sentinel might be seen watching the progress of the troops, but flying at the slightest motion of anyone towards him, naturally supposing, from the treatment he and his friends had experienced from their own troops, that little mercy would be shown by strangers.

In the direction of Tonghoo, the column marched to Tagoondine, forty miles east of Prome, and situated at the bottom of the Galadzet mountains, To this point an easterly movement was necessarily limited, the rains setting in, and the numerous dry rivulets we had crossed on our route, already threatening an early change to deep rivers and mountain torrents, precluding all hope of returning to Prome by that road, had an advance been persevered in: a small party, however, was ordered to ascend the pass over the mountains, which was found so steep and rugged, as to offer serious obstacles to the passage of an army.

These bleak and sterile mountains are thinly inhabited by Krayns, a tribe of innocent, but hideous looking mountaineers, from the practice that prevails among them of tattooing their faces, especially the women, whose uncouth and frightful countenances must require the full benefit of long established custom and habit, or religious prejudice, to enable even a Krayn to regard them with other feelings than those of horror and disgust.

After passing the mountains, the road leads through a desert and dreary waste, with a few miserable cottages scattered over it, until within a day's march of Tonghoo, when the country assumes a more cultivated appearance; but as it is yet only known from the report of natives, little faith can be placed in their extravagant accounts. It is said to be the second city in the empire, and surrounded by a brick wall, and ditch, of some strength. It was formerly the capital of an independent kingdom, and is now the jaghire (or estate) of the king's eldest brother, who also bears the title of Prince of Tonghoo.

From Tagoondine, the column moved upon the Irrawaddy, towards Meaday, occasionally crossing the route by which corps of the Burmese army had retired from Prome. It was painful to witness the ruinous effects of their system of warfare: even Russia, in her memorable resistance to the armies of Napoleon, did not offer to the invading host such a continued scene of desolation: neither man nor beast escaped the retiring columns; and heaps of ashes, with groups of hungry, howling dogs, alone indicated where villages had been.

Meaday, once a town of considerable magnitude and importance, was completely destroyed by fire; scarcely a vestige of the place remained. Its old brick wall appeared to have been recently cleared and strengthened by breastworks and stockading; but no one remained to give intelligence of the enemy's movements, or when he had retreated: indeed, to judge by the state of the country, one might have supposed that resistance was at an end, and that its population, retiring in a body to the north, had quietly relinquished the southern provinces to the invaders, leaving behind them a broad and desolate region, as a future barrier and frontier.

The column now commenced its retrograde march upon Prome, giving assurances of protection and kind treatment to such villages as were found inhabited on its march back, along the banks of the river. In some instances the villagers were discovered with all their cattle, and property, living in the jungles, and induced to return to their homes; but by far the greater number had been driven to a distance by the armed police, whose especial duty it was to guard against our receiving aid or assistance of any kind from the districts through which we marched.

Chapter 16

Consolidation

The setting in of the rainy season, early in June, closed the operations of the campaign. Cantonments, for the reception of the troops, were speedily prepared in the neighbourhood of Prome; and every encouragement was held out to the terrified natives who had either fled to the jungle, or been driven away by their army, to return to their deserted homes. Their houses were left unoccupied; their little property scrupulously taken care of; and proclamations, inviting them to return, and promising protection, and liberal payment for the fruits of their industry, were distributed as much as possible throughout the country.

The happy result of these measures exceeded our most sanguine expectations. The persecuted inhabitants poured in from every quarter; some from the woods, bringing their families, cattle, wagons, and other property along with them; but by far the greater number had escaped: from military escorts, and returned in a most miserable and starving condition, having lost or been plundered by their guards of everything belonging to them. It is, happily, not in the nature of a Burmese to despond, or long repine at past sufferings or losses; contentment, and a cheerful acquiescence in the decrees of fate, seldom abandon him and those who had the good luck to find their houses undestroyed were, in a few hours, comfortably established: while their less fortunate companions, whose abodes had perished in the conflagration, applied themselves with such zeal and assiduity to the construction of their light and airy habitations, that, in the course of a few weeks, Prome had not only recovered from the desolating effects of the system pursued by the Burmese leaders, but had risen from its ashes in greater magnitude than it could boast of, even in its proudest days.

The tide of population long receding before us, having once overcome the barrier that restrained it, now flowed back into the deserted provinces; the natives retiring from the vicinity and approach of their own armies to seek for safety and protection under the British flag; dying from the oppressive measures and arbitrary exactions of their own government, to seek for peace and an industrious livelihood in the cantonments of a foreign enemy. Plentiful bazaars, at every Station, soon. bore ample testimony to the confidence of the inhabitants in the justice and good faith of their invaders, whose troops now lived in comfort and abundance, enjoying themselves in unmolested ease, after the fatigues and privations of an arduous, though short, campaign; and presenting a striking contrast to the miserable and ill-conducted armies of the King of Ava, who, unpaid, unsupplied, and trusting wholly for resources to what they could extort or seize from the industrious and labouring peasantry. were now frequently reduced to the. alternative of choosing between dispersion and starvation.

The towns and districts in our rear following the example of the provincial capital, we had soon the satisfaction of seeing the banks of the Irrawaddy, under Prome, enlivened by the presence of a happy and contented people, whose only care and anxiety arose from the apprehension of our departure, and their consequent re-subjection to their former masters. But gratifying in every way as was the change ·which had taken place in the sentiments of the people towards us, and as pleasing as was the comfortable appearance of a well-supplied bazaar, crowded town, and quiet country, contrasted with the picture of our last winter-quarters at Rangoon, it is chiefly in a military point of view, that the measures of the leader, and the discipline and good conduct of the troops, which had produced these consequences, are to be prized; for, independent of the; preservation of health among the troops, in itself an object of no small moment, the army was deficient in adequate conveyance for supplies from our Rangoon stores, and totally unprovided with equipment for prosecuting the war at the return of the cold season; and from local means alone, with the active and zealous aid of the people, could we hope to remedy these deficiencies.

The first thing to be attended to, was the formation of a depot at Prome, without which we could neither move in advance, nor even hope to maintain, for any length of time, the commanding situation then occupied by the army. Liberal payment, on such occasions, is generally the most eloquent appeal that can be made upon men of all nations; but to a Burmese, especially, unused to receive anything but stripes for his labour, it may be supposed our mode of treating those who served us, had peculiar charms.

Large fleets of canoes, so constructed as to stem the torrents of the Irrawaddy, were soon placed at the disposal of the commissariat, and such a stock of provisions conveyed to, and kept up at Prome, as was judged adequate for supplying the force in an advance upon the capital.

The next object to be secured, was the purchase of a sufficient number of carts and cattle for the conveyance of commissariat stores, and the equipment of the foot-artillery in the ensuing campaign; and although, during our march, few cattle had been seen, it was well known that the Prome district and higher parts of Pegu abounded in herds of the finest description: the religion of the Burmese forbidding their putting to death: any domestic animal, cows and oxen are used exclusively for labour, and are only liable to die from sickness or old age. The people were scarcely settled in their houses, when the plains which we had traversed, without finding even the means of provisioning the men, were again covered with numerous herds; from every pathway of the deep and extensive forests, that everywhere throughout the kingdom usurp more than half the soil, droves of the finest oxen now daily issued; and the country, which we had hitherto found so poor and destitute of the means of supporting an army, was suddenly become rich and fertile in resources for sustaining and prosecuting the most protracted warfare. The troops were rationed from cattle sold expressly for that purpose by the natives, who, although themselves forbidden to slaughter them, were not offended in any of their religious prejudices by their being killed by strangers, but, on the contrary, were always ready to partake even of those parts which were rejected as offal by the purchasers. Draught and carriage oxen were at the same time bought in sufficient numbers to equip the force for service in the field.

But to secure the full benefit of the return of the inhabitants to their villages, it was necessary to guard against anarchy and confusion, by organizing some system of native government for the conquered provinces; and without making any material alteration in the form that had prevailed previous to our arrival, an arrangement was adopted, which secured to us every desirable advantage—maintained order and regularity among the people, while it protected them from the exercise of any wanton acts of authority on the part of their chiefs, who were deprived of the arbitrary power vested in them, and so cruelly displayed under their former masters.

The Burmese empire is divided into provinces and districts of very unequal magnitude and importance; these divisions are separately governed by a military chief or viceroy, called Maywoon, who is aided in his duties by one or more subordinate chiefs, called Raywoons, according to the size of his command. These form the provincial lotoo, or council, in which is vested the power of life and death over everyone within its jurisdiction; for, although by law any subject may appeal from its decree to the council of state, or grand lotoo, at Ava, the difficulty and expense of making the reference are so great as to render the privilege nearly nominal. These governors and military chiefs have no salary from the crown, but are allowed certain fees on all law-suits, an item of certain taxes, and may extort and levy contributions at pleasure on all under their control.

When the king makes war, assembles forces, or, as in the present instance, the kingdom is invaded, it is the duty of the Maywoons to raise the quota of men the province may be required to furnish, and to levy such extraordinary taxes for their equipment .and supplies as the occasion may require. Such opportunities afford a rich harvest to the rapacity of these petty despots, as they generally take care to raise double the number of men that may be ordered, allowing one-half to buy their discharge, according to their means; and pocketing at least half the amount of what is collected for the equipment of the other. Such is the general character of the military governors of the Burmese provinces, with whom of course no intercourse took place; their interest bound them too firmly to their master to be drawn into any connexion with his enemy.

But there is another and a better, though a subordinate class of chiefs, who stand in a very different relation to the crown; and who were found ready to fill the situations so much required, to maintain order and peace among the daily increasing population of the conquered territory. These were the Meuthogees, or civil chiefs, of whom there is one in every town and district in the empire. The situation of Meuthogee is generally hereditary, and has considerable power and importance vested in it; and although in every respect inferior and subordinate to the Maywoons and their officers, the Meuthogees, nevertheless, enjoy a large share of influence in the management of their respective ·districts: through them the taxes are collected, and the orders of the viceroy promulgated and carried into effect. They are also permitted to hold courts for the trial of petty cases; and the law, that fertile source from which so many in every land draw subsistence, to them also affords a principal item of their fees of office.

These men, unlike their military superiors, whose post was in the field, at the head of the armed contingent of the province, generally remained in charge of their respective districts, forwarding to the army its resources in men and money, as occasion required, or as the arbitrary and inflexible commands of the absent governor directed. Once freed from the control of their own government by the advance of the British army, the Meuthogees, returning at the head of their people from the woods, readily accepted of employment, and were regularly installed in their former dignties and offices, deprived, however, of all arbitrary power, and forbidden to punish beyond a limited imprisonment, without the sanction of the British authorities, to whom the proceedings of all criminal or serious cases were to be forwarded for examination and approval; and it is a fact, not unworthy of remark, that during the stay of the army at Prome, surrounded by an immense population, with the country naturally in an agitated and unsettled state, only one instance of capital punishment took place, and the individual was a native, convicted of robbery and murder.

Taxes being abolished, and abundance of money in circulation, happiness and plenty prevailed among all classes of society: even the reinstated chiefs were delighted with the change, although by it they had lost, what long custom bad taught them to consider as a right, the pillaging of the people, under the constant, varied, and ever arbitrary exactions of their own discretion. In the new arrangements, fees, or a certain percentage on all ·law-suits, was alone continued to them; but as the Burmese, notwithstanding the iniquitous practices of their courts of law, are rather fond of litigation, and as money was now plentiful among them, there is reason to think that the emoluments of the Meuthogees were not much reduced by the change, and, at all events, they were now free from former heavy grievances—the liability of being in their turn plundered by their superiors. But, however imperfect and inadequate to the purposes of good government the system may appear, it must be allowed, that, considered merely as a temporary measure, it relieved the people from a load of misery and oppression, and fully answered all the purposes for which it was intended, maintaining peace and quietness in the country, and ensuring regular supplies and aid of every description to the army; neither interfering materially with the customs or prejudices of the natives, while it gradually and imperceptibly opened their eyes to the cruelties and tyranny of their iniquitous oppressors, and prepared them, it may be hoped, for the reception, at no very distant period, of a more enlightened form of government; and may ultimately lead to the civilization and moral improvement of a people highly favoured by nature, and naturally shrewd, intelligent, and brave.

Unshackled by the caste of the Hindoo, or the creed of the intolerant Mussulman, but free from religious prejudice, and proud of himself and of the land that gave him birth, the Burmese is ready to receive any change which would tend to raise him in the scale of civilized society; so slight, indeed, is their regard for their present code of worship, that it has often been remarked, and not without strong and weighty reason, that the king of Ava, could, by a simple order, change the religion of the nation without a murmur being heard.

Five months of uninterrupted tranquillity gave us, for the first time, an opportunity of forming some acquaintance with the manners and customs of the people of Ava; and although some allowance must fairly be made for the restraint, which the presence of a victorious enemy may be presumed to have imposed upon the development of the national character, our experience, at least, warrants the assertion, that in his private and domestic habits and deportment, the Burmese evinces little of the arrogance, cruelty, or vice, which have made him so justly an object of fear and hatred to the surrounding nations, to whom he is only known as a sanguinary and ferocious warrior, carrying havoc and destruction into *free* and unoffending states, at the command of a grasping and ambitious tyrant.

Born a soldier, the Burmese is accustomed, from his earliest years, to consider war and foreign conquest as his trade, and the plunder of the countries he invades as the fair and legitimate reward of his toil: he seldom gives or receives quarter from his enemies; and while on foreign service, is ever but too ready to execute the cruel orders of his chiefs, whose policy it is to extirpate all who are likely to be troublesome, and to impress those, whom policy leads them to spare, with a wholesome and deep-rooted terror for the Burmhan arms. Guided by leaders, whose barbarous ideas of successful warfare consist in laying waste an enemy's country, and whose fame and rewards are measured by the numbers of the enemy that are slain or carried into bondage, it too frequently follows, that the soldiers, leaving the best and kindest feelings of their heart in the cottage that contains their family, and forgetting every feeling of humanity, as a duty, pursue, with reckless indifference, every species of cruelty and excess, among the unfortunate people, who have experienced the awful visitation of a Burmese army.

When engaged in offensive warfare, which in their native quarrels has generally been the case, the Burmese is arrogant, bold, and daring: possessed of strength and activity superior to all his neighbours, and capable of enduring great fatigue, his movements are rapid, and his perseverance in overcoming obstacles, almost irresistible: possessed, too, of superior science and ability in their peculiar system of fighting, he had seldom met his equal in the field, or even experienced serious resistance in the numerous conquests which of late years had been added to the empire, until the increasing arrogance and aggressions of his government brought him, at last, in contact with an enemy of a very different description from any he had yet contended with, and presented his military character in a different light, divested of the glare which victory and success had long shed around it.

The occurrences at Rangoon afford a pretty fair specimen of the vigour and harassing assiduity with which they commenced the contest with the British troops: nor did their spirit fail them, until they had seen their best generals killed, their strongest, and, as they imagined, impregnable stockades and defences taken with the greatest ease, the sacred prophecies of their astrologers unfulfilled, and half their country in the hands of their enemy—then, indeed, they began to feel that they were vanquished; all confidence in themselves and in their chiefs was lost; and neither the money nor the authority of the king could longer convince them, that they were still a match for British soldiers. Still, men were found and armies formed, to support the despot's cause; but although they sometimes offered a brave resistance to their foes, they no longer fought with that fury which had at first distinguished them; and when chance threw an unfortunate prisoner into their hands, he was not now put to death in cold blood, but treated with mercy and even kindness. The fear of retaliation had so far produced a salutary change in their barbarous customs, which the example of forbearance in their opponents would never have effected.

Our previous opinion of, and limited acquaintance with the people, certainly had not prepared us to anticipate the tranquil and quiet conduct which ·now distinguished them in their domestic character; nor was the Prome population exclusively composed of the quiet and unwarlike part of the nation: many, indeed, a great proportion of the men had borne arms against us; and it was not until satisfied of the folly and vanity of contending longer, that .they had escaped from their chiefs, and retired, with their families, under our protection.

At home, the Burmese, probably owing to his military habits, is decidedly lazy, and averse to work—to his shame, allowing, or rather compelling his wife to toil hard for the support of his family, while he passes his time in idleness, smoking, or chewing betel, the favourite pastime of natives of all ranks: his wants, however are few and simple; rice, and a little pickled fish constitute the chief articles of food, while water is his only drink:

naturally good-humoured and contented, he seems happy and resigned, bearing all the oppressions, to which he may be subjected, with apathy and indifference; and in his own house he is kind and affectionate to his children, seldom evincing anger or ill-treatment to any member of his family.

It must, however, be allowed, that the Burmese are little guided or restrained in their conduct and actions by any moral principle: selling their daughters, even to strangers, is a common practice among them; nor does the transaction reflect either disgrace or shame on the parties concerned. Government, upon political grounds, strictly prohibits any woman from being allowed to leave the country; and the unhappy females, who are sacrificed to this disgraceful custom, generally return to their families, in no way slighted or degraded, but more frequently, as objects of envy, from the little stock of wealth they bring back with them.

It has often been objected to the Burmese, that they are given to pilfering, lying, and dissimulation, as well as insolent and overbearing to strangers; but the remark may be, in a great measure, confined to the numerous government functionaries and their followers, with whom every town and village in the kingdom abounds: they are indeed a vile race, who exist by fraud and oppression, and who, upon numerous pretences, no matter how frivolous, are always ready to rob and plunder all who come within the influence of their authority: the poor people, on the contrary, by far the best part of the nation, are frank and hospitable, and by no means deficient in qualities which would do honour to more civilized nations. They, very generally, can read and write; are acute, intelligent, and observing; and, although frequently impressed with high notions of their own sovereign and country, show no illiberality to strangers or foreigners who reside among them. In a word, to sum up their character, their virtues are their own, and their faults and vices those of education, and the pernicious influence of a cruel and despotic government.

In Ava all rank is official, emanating from, and continued

or suspended at the will or caprice of the sovereign; and the lowest Burmese, if possessed of talent, may aspire to the highest situation in the realm: it is, consequently, no uncommon thing to see, at this despotic court, a man holding, one day, offices of the highest trust and honour, and the next, stripped of his chain and badge, and degraded to a level with the poorest of the people, considering himself fortunate that his head was not also forfeited to his loss of favour in the Golden Palace.

It is impossible to conceive a quieter or happier town than Prome continued during the stay of the British forces. To the inhabitants it was altogether a new life, to be treated kindly, and receive payment for their services and the fruits of their industry. The troops, in the meantime, undisturbed by any enemy, continued healthy and robust. The Irrawaddy was our only hostile visitor during the rains, making occasional inroads upon our cantonments, overflowing its embankments, and inundating the town and surrounding plains—driving several corps, whose quarters were not sufficiently elevated, to the heights above the town, where experience finally taught us they were alone safe from its sudden and impetuous irruptions. The inhabitants, a half amphibious race, viewed the rushing torrent with indifference: accustomed to its annual visit, and knowing the utmost limit of its greatest encroachment, they could not conceive, why people, provided with houses raised on piles, should feel uncomfortable in their aquatic abodes. To them the change is pleasing, perhaps useful, in cleansing their towns from the accumulated filth and rubbish of eight months' collection.

When the waters rise, numerous little canoes are called into general use, in which the people go about their usual occupations without fear or inconvenience; but by us, who felt the tedium and annoyance of confinement and inactivity, the reflux of the river within its usual boundaries, and the approaching return of the dry season, was hailed with general delight.

CHAPTER 17

Negotations

The season of rest and inactivity was not spent by the court of Ava in profitless sorrow for their recent losses, nor in any attempt to rid the country of our presence, by negotiation. Undismayed by the threatening attitude of the British force, concession was still far from the mind of the infatuated king, and his advisers: the overtures of the British general were treated with silent contempt and the most vigorous measures were once more adopted, in the hope of checking our farther progress, and of finally wearying us out in the protracted contest.

Men were levied in every part of the kingdom, and, to insure their fidelity, large bounties were given—a thing formerly unheard of, and unknown among them. The arsenals were kept in constant employment, making powder, repairing old arms, and preparing new; such as jingals and wall-pieces, with the manufacturing of which they are well acquainted. Orders were, at the same time, sent to the tributary Shan tribes, bordering on China, to furnish their quotas in the present emergency; and an armed contingent, of fifteen thousand men, was embodied, disciplined, and headed by their chiefs, or Chobwas, marched forward to the capital, from these distant states.

Unacquainted with the progress of the war, and filled with extravagant ideas of the power and invincible courage of their conquerors, they readily obeyed the imperial mandate, in the hope of sharing the wealth and honour which had been abundantly promised to them in the defeat of the strangers, whose presumption had led them into a situation from whence escape was hopeless. In language to this effect, the Lotoo continued to address and dupe the more distant. parts of the country, where the real situation of affairs was still unknown, with so much success, that, before the end of September, a disposable force, of not less than seventy thousand men, was in readiness to-oppose the different columns, which threatened an advance upon the capital.

No expense was spared, or promise of reward forgotten, to rouse the spirit of the soldier, and stimulate him to exertion: quantities of muskets, which had long been hoarded up in store in Ava were now liberally distributed. The equipment of this force was also rendered more complete: the whole collected power of Ava seemed to be forming in array against us, and shed a last gleam of hope around the declining fortunes of the Burmhan monarch, who, cheered by delusive prospects, and confident in the imposing magnitude of his preparations, at length empowered his generals to listen and reply to any pacific communications that might in future be received, and to open negotiations, if the English wished it; not as a vanquished nation ready to make concessions, but as delegates from a formidable army, to ascertain if we were yet weary of the contest, and disposed to give it up on friendly terms, as a matter of expediency and mutual interest.

In the beginning of October, the headquarters of the Burmese army were again at Meaday, upon which place the different corps were rapidly concentrating, when, in answer to a letter, that had some time previously been sent from the British headquarters, representing the ruinous consequences to the King of Ava of further prolongation of the war, and urging the Burmese chiefs to consult the true interest of their sovereign, by listening to the lenient terms of peace that were still offered to their acceptance, a complimentary mission was sent to Prome, charged, as they expressed themselves, to speak many good words, and to state the desire and anxiety of the king, and his ministers, for a lasting peace between the two great nations.

In return for this compliment, two British officers were despatched to Meaday, where they were received by the Kee Wongee, or Prime Minister, to whom they were directed to offer an armistice and propose a meeting between duly-authorised commissioners from the respective armies.

The armistice was accepted of, and it was agreed that the Kee Wongee, and another chief, named Lamain Woon, should meet the British general half way between the two armies, at a; place named Neoun-ben-zeik; each party to be escorted by six hundred men, the rank of the Kee Wongee not permitting him to move with a smaller escort. These preliminaries being settled, the officers returned. to Prome; and on the day appointed, the commissioners, with their respective guards, were encamped upon the plain of Neoun-ben-zeik, at the distance of nearly a mile asunder; and in the intermediate space, equidistant from both camps, a house had been prepared as a place of conference. The necessary arrangements and formalities of the meeting were then stipulated for, by subordinate officers, with the most scrupulous exactness, tenaciously adhering to the most trivial points of form, and carefully guarding against anything that might be construed into an acknowledgment of the slightest inferiority.

At length, all points being satisfactorily adjusted, both parties, leaving camp at the same moment, met in front of the conference house, where shaking of hands and every demonstration of amicable feeling having passed, the parties entered the house, and sat down on two rows of chairs fronting each other: the Wongees, and their suite, in all fifteen chiefs, each bearing the chain of nobility, and dressed in their splendid court-dresses, evidently doing grievous penance in seats they had never been accustomed to, that no difference might appear, even in the most trifling particular between the parties;

and so observing and tenacious were they on this paint, that scarcely a movement could be made without a corresponding one on their side; and their great aim seemed to be to show the most perfect knowledge of our customs and manners.

After many kind inquiries for the King, and royal family of England, in which every allusion to the Governor-General and East India Company was carefully avoided, the Wongees requested that negotiations might be suspended, and all business deferred till the following day, that a better acquaintance might be formed before entering on the important subject for which they were assembled, confining themselves, on the present occasion, to general expressions of regard and desire for peace; regretting that two such great and enlightened nations should unfortunately have been engaged in war through mistake, or misunderstanding.

On the following day, the same forms being gone through, Sir Archibald Campbell at once opened the business, by a brief recapitulation of the unprovoked aggressions which had obliged the Indian government, after many fruitless endeavours to gain redress by milder measures, to appeal to arms in vindication of their invaded rights and insulted territory; and of the success that had crowned their efforts by the conquest of the best half of the Burmese dominions. The imposing situation and formidable strength of the British force, threatening the subjugation of the capital, was then alluded to, concluding with a statement of the terms upon which he was empowered to sign a peace, and at once evacuate the country with his army.

The Kee Wongee and his colleague replied, that the aggressions we complained of were unauthorised by the Burmese government, and entirely owing to the unwarrantable conduct of three bad men, who were employed in Arracan, and had kept back the letters and remonstrances of the Indian government from the knowledge of the King—with many other frivolous and absurd excuses, in which a scrupulous regard to truth was little attended to, as was fully proved to them, without, in any way, affronting or offending their feelings—truth being by them scarcely rated as a virtue.

They then tried various methods of inducing the British general to withdraw the principal demands, stating the advantages we should derive as a mercantile nation, by a friendly accommodation with them; that it might cost them their heads to show such terms as were offered, to the King; and, finally, proposing that the business should be settled, as they had formerly concluded a peace nearly in similar circumstances, with the Chinese, by forgetting the past and pledging mutual friendship for the future; and that although the dignity and most sacred customs of the nation alike forbade the King of Ava to accede to any terms imposed upon, or dictated to, him, that when the British army should have left the country, there was nothing we could ask, that he, out of the generosity of his heart, would not cheerfully bestow.

When told that history gave a very different termination to the Chinese war*, they laughed heartily at being detected by our knowledge of the fact; and after long discussions, and trying every expedient to induce a modification, finding the British general firm and unbending in his proposals, they at last requested that a prolongation of the armistice for twenty days might be granted, to enable them to forward the terms to Ava, and receive His Majesty's commands upon the subject. Notwithstanding the apparent desire for peace, so well supported by the Burmhan chiefs, it was but too evident, from the very first, that the negotiations would lead to nothing; and although it was also pretty certain that a reference to Ava would in no way amend the matter, a renewed armistice was readily granted—the advantage being wholly on our side, as the season would not yet admit of any movement, while the never-idle Burmese marauding bands might be restrained from annoying us, during the period we were still necessarily confined to quarters.

---

*The Chinese army, which invaded Ava, having been routed and literally -put to the sword.

One important point was, however, gained in opening a communication with the court of Ava and establishing a degree of confidence in the honour and integrity of our dealings, which neither the habits nor experience of the Burmese chiefs had prepared them for, nor their intentions in opening negotiations, led them to expect; indeed, it required every effort of kindness and judgment to impress upon their suspicious and deceitful minds, that the Indian government was really desirous of terminating, what they naturally conceived was, to us, an advantageous contest, or that the leaders of a victorious army could be sincere in their pacific professions. Accustomed to fight solely for plunder and the aggrandisement of the kingdom, without regard to justice, or idea of peace, while they continue successful, and anything is to be gained, they could not readily admit the belief of our voluntarily relinquishing conquests which had cost so much blood and expense in acquiring; it is, on the contrary, much more probable that the communications which led to the meeting, were by them attributed to weakness, and answered, in the hope of gaining some insight into our situation, or other advantage, by dissimulation and intrigue. To them, an offer to treat was, perhaps, considered tantamount to an acknowledgment, either that we felt ourselves unable to prosecute the war—to retain our situation in the country, or that, from some cause or other unknown to them, we were under the necessity of abandoning our acquisitions on the best terms we could, or at all-events prepared to grant a much more favourable arrangement than we had yet proposed—in whichever case something might be hoped from their skill and cunning as negotiators.

With some such sentiments and views as these, there can be but little doubt the conference was granted; and if the meeting did no more than remove the erroneous opinion they had formed, of the motives which actuated government, in making them such liberal proposals, a most important point was gained, in inspiring trust and confidence in our promises and dealings, and in opening the road to a future accommodation: they had an opportunity of undeceiving themselves regarding the supposed influence and value of their diplomatic talents; a closer view satisfied them that their enemy was neither guided nor affected by the same rules, customs or habits, which regulated their own conduct.

Nothing was more striking during the conference than the anxiety of the chiefs to show themselves well acquainted with the manners and customs of European nations, and of their own claim to rank in every respect as high as any of them in the scale of society—taking every opportunity of repeating the words in allusion to their own country, and England, "The two great and civilized nations," reprobating the putting to death of prisoners, and many other barbarous acts they are in the constant practice of. Upon the whole, however, they conducted themselves with much discretion and good-humour, and we parted on. the most friendly terms: they dined with Sir Archibald Campbell, previous to their departure, comporting themselves at table with ease and propriety, narrowly observing every motion of their entertainers, and showing amazing quickness in following their example. They freely partook of everything on the table; a ham in particular: seemed to be much relished, and at the Kee Wongee's request, was made over to him in a present; but either from taste, or respect to the orders of the King, which forbid the use of wine and spirituous liquors, they drank sparingly, once or twice only filling their glasses to the toasts that were proposed.

It may be questioned, whether or not their lordships would have been so abstemious in private, as the lower orders are so excessively fond of liquor of every description, that they never hesitate, when in their power, to disobey an order, the penalty of which is death. On parting, the Wongees again repeated their anxious desire for peace*, said their best endeavours

---

*Among ourselves, many believed that the war was at an end, while others could not forget that we were dealing with a government proverbially false, and so completely influenced and guided by signs and omens, that an unusual grunt from the white elephant was at all times sufficient to interrupt the most important affairs, and cause the most solemn engagements to be broken off.

would be used to effect that desirable object, and expressed a strong hope that they would be crowned with success.

A few days, however, served to prove the fallacy of these expectations; for scarcely had we reached Prome on our return, when reports poured in from all quarters of the irruption of numerous predatory bands from the Burmese army over the line of demarcation into the districts under our protection, burning, plundering, and laying waste the country up to the very gates of Prome, cutting off the supplies coming up the river for the army, and threatening wholly to intercept our communication with Rangoon and the rear—in direct violation of the specified and clearly-understood terms of the armistice. Repeated remonstrances on the subject were sent in vain to the Burmese leaders: they strenuously denied all knowledge of, and connexion with the marauders, in the face of the dearest evidence that they were acting under immediate authority from the headquarters of their army, as proved by all the prisoners taken by our patrols.

Finally, towards the expiration of the armistice, a definite answer was received to the proffered terms, couched in the following laconic terms: "If you wish for peace, you may go away; but if you ask either money or territory, no friendship can exist between us. This is Burmhan custom!!!"

This haughty declaration was immediately followed by a general advance from Meaday.

CHAPTER 18

Hard Fighting

In obedience to the most peremptory orders received from Ava, to surround and attack the rebel strangers on all sides, the Burmese forces advanced upon Prome in three divisions; the right, under the command of Sudda Woon, consisting of fifteen thousand men, having crossed the Ir-rawaddy, moved forward upon its west bank, detaching a corps to its front, for the purpose of intercepting our communication with the rear; the centre, of from twenty-five to thirty thousand strong, commanded by the Kee Wongee in person, moved along the east or left bank of the river, accompanied by a considerable fleet of war-boats, escorting the commissariat and other stores of the army; the left division, also fifteen thousand strong, was led by Maha Nemiow, an old and experienced general, lately arrived from court, with express authority for directing the general operations of the army; this corps moved by a route about ten miles distant from the river, from which it was separated by an extensive forest running parallel to the river for the distance of twenty miles, also several miles in depth, and so thick and impervious as to form an impassable barrier between the left and centre, but leaving each exposed to a separate attack without the benefit of mutual co-operation or assistance.

In addition to these three corps, a reserve of ten thousand men, commanded by the king's half-brother, Prince Memiaboo, occupied a strongly-fortified post at Melloone; another force was in readiness to oppose any movement from Arracan, and Sykia Wonghee, with Ondinah, the ex-rajah of Martaban, still carried on a desultory warfare in the neighbourhood of old Pegu, occasionally threatening an attack upon Rangoon.

The effective British force destined to overcome these formidable preparations, and assembled at Prome, consisted of eight weak British regiments, six battalions of Madras Native Infantry, one troop of dragoons, and a considerable train of horse and foot artillery; leaving, after garrisoning Prome, a field force of about five thousand men, of which three thousand were British. Three corps of Native Infantry, and a Company's European regiment, were opposed to Sykia Wongee, in Pegu, and ordered by Sir Archibald Campbell, if sufficient equipment could be obtained, to make a forward movement upon Tonghoo.* Rangoon was also occupied by a British regiment, and a considerable force of native infantry. Spies and assassin emissaries were again at work within our lines at Prome, increasing our anxiety for an early meeting with the enemy.

About the 10th of November, the advance of Maha Nemiow's corps took post at Watty-goon, distant from Prome about sixteen miles, in a N.E. direction, threatening to turn our position by its right, with a view to taking post in our rear, and throwing reinforcements into Pegu, measures which would have rendered the situation of the British force extremely embarrassing, and a forward movement, with its communication and supplies thus intercepted, hazardous and ineffectual. Two brigades of Native infantry, under Colonel M'Dowall, of the Madras army, were therefore ordered to dislodge the enemy from Watty-goon; one brigade moving by a central road towards that place, and the other two corps marching by circuitous routes, arranged so as to reach the scene of action at the same moment, and assail the enemy in flank and rear, while he was attacked in front by the main body. The Burmese, obtaining information of the move-

---

* Or Taunu

146

ment, did not wait to be visited in their position; but meeting the columns about half way, commenced an animated and continued skirmish with our troops, through a difficult, enclosed country, showing considerable bodies of Cassay horse, as often as the roads emerged from the jungle into the plain, and completely frustrating the simultaneous arrival and combined attack of the three corps. The centre, driving the enemy before them, at length reached Watty-goon, which was found to be stockaded; and Colonel M'Dowall, while reconnoitring the place, being unfortunately killed, the other corps not making their appearance, and the enemy appearing much too numerous to be dislodged without their aid, a retreat was ordered, and conducted with steadiness and regularity; though not without severe loss, the enemy closely following it up for several miles.

Emboldened by their success, Maha Nemiow changed his line of operations, advancing direct upon Prome, but pursuing the same cautious plan of approach, moving slowly, and stockading himself at every mile, as he advanced. A corresponding movement to the front being made by the other divisions of the Burmese army, the centre was now distinctly seen from Prome, stockading and fortifying the heights of Napadee above the river, distant only five miles. The corps of Sudda Woon was also seen actively employed in a similar duty on the opposite bank, while a strong detachment was pushed forward for the purpose of occupying Padoung-mew, a town situated on the west side of the Irrawaddy, about ten miles below Prome: in this measure, however, they were anticipated by the British general, the place being already in possession of a party of our troops, which subsequently baffled every attempt of the enemy to drive them from it.

Every day now produced a change in the Burmese line; working incessantly, night and day, each morning discovered to us some new work in front of where their advanced parties had been posted on the preceding evening. It seemed to be the intention of the veteran chief, who now directed matters, not to risk his reputation, and perhaps his head, by any rash attempt which might lead to failure, but to push his approaches so near that a simultaneous and overwhelming rush might be made from all sides upon the British force. He appears to have succeeded in inspiring his men with great confidence and spirit; and his astrologers had foretold that an approaching lunar eclipse would undoubtedly prove a favourable time for commencing his attack. To encourage him as much as possible to grant a meeting in every way so desirable, our troops were kept cautiously within their lines, making batteries, and throwing up entrenchments, as if apprehensive of a visit from their formidable opponents; and rumours were even circulated, that preparations were in progress for retiring suddenly by water to Rangoon; even that, however, failed to accelerate the business, or to lead the wary leader into the slightest indiscretion. He knew too well the materials of which his army was composed, to trust it in the plain before a disciplined force, however inferior in numbers; and seemed resolved to adhere most scrupulously to the slow but safe stockading and entrenching system, which, in his earlier years, had so often crowned his efforts with success.

Seeing little prospect of a speedy crisis to the cautious tactics of his adversary, suffering from the depredations of the enemy's detached parties upon our river convoys, and anxious that not a day of the short season of active operations should be lost, Sir Archibald Campbell resolved to wait no longer, but, as the enemy was now within his reach, at once to become the assailant.

The corps of Maha Nemiow had for some days remained stationary within a morning's walk of Prome, assiduously occupied in strengthening their hidden position in the jungles of Simbike and Kyalaz, on the Nawine river, maintaining so close and vigilant a watch, and conducting matters with so much secrecy, as to prevent us from gaining the slightest information either as to the extent or nature of their defences, or the intention of their leader, when finished. Eight thousand men of his *corps d'armee* were Shans, who had not yet come in contact with our troops, and were expected to fight with more spirit, and resolution than those who had a more intimate acquaintance with their enemy. In addition to a numerous host of Chobwas and petty princes, these levies were accompanied by three young and handsome women of high rank, who were believed, by their superstitious countrymen, to be endowed not only with the gift of prophecy and foreknowledge, but to possess the miraculous power of turning aside the balls of the English, rendering them wholly innocent and harmless. These Amazons, dressed in warlike costume, rode constantly among the troops, inspiring them with courage and ardent wishes for an early meeting with their foe, as yet only known to them by the deceitful accounts of their Burmese masters.

On the 30th of November arrangements: were made for attacking the enemy on the following morning, beginning with the left, and taking the three *corps d'armee* rapidly in detail, which their insulated situation afforded every facility for doing. Commodore Sir James Brisbane, with the flotilla, was to commence a cannonade upon the enemy's posts, upon both banks of the Irrawaddy, at daylight, and a body of Native infantry was at the same time to advance along the margin of the river, upon the Kee Wongee's position at Napadee, and to drive in his advanced posts upon the main body, drawing the enemy's whole attention to his right and centre, while the columns were marching out for the real attack upon the left, at Simbike. Leaving four regiments of Native infantry in garrison, at daylight, on the morning of the 1st of December, the rest of the force was assembled, and formed in two columns of attack at a short distance in front of Prome; one, under Brigadier-General Cotton, marched by the straight road leading to Simbike, while the other, accompanied by the commander of the forces, crossed the Nawine river, moving along its right bank, for the purpose of attacking the enemy in the rear, and cutting off his retreat upon the Kee Wongee's division.

The columns had scarcely moved off, when a furious cannonade upon our left announced the commencement of operations on the river, and so completely deceived the enemy, that we found the piquets of his left with drawn, and the position at Simbike exposed to a sudden and unexpected attack. Brigadier-General Cotton's column first reached the enemy's line, consisting of a succession of stockades erected across an open space in the centre of the jungle, where the villages of Simbike and Kyalay had stood, having the Nawine river in the rear, a thick wood on either flank, and assailable only by the open space in front, defended by cross-fires from the zigzagging formation of the works. The Brigadier-General having quickly made his dispositions, the troops, consisting of His Majesty's Forty-First in front, and the flank companies of His Majesty's Royal and Eighty-Ninth regiments, with the eighteenth Madras Native Infantry in flank, moved forward with their usual intrepidity; the Shans, encouraged by the presence of their veteran commander, who, unable to walk, was carried from point to point, in a handsomely-gilded litter; and cheered by the example, and earnest exhortations to fight bravely, of the fearless Amazons, offered a brave resistance to the assailants; but no sooner was a lodgement made in the interior of their crowded works, than confusion ensued, and they were unable longer to contend with, or check the progress of the rapidly-increasing line which formed upon their ramparts, and from whose destructive vollies there was no escaping: the strongly-built enclosures, of their own construction, everywhere preventing flight, dead and dying blocked up the few and narrow outlets from the work. Horses and men ran in wild confusion from side to side, trying to avoid the fatal fire; groups were employed in breaking down, and trying to force a passage through the defences, while the brave, who disdained to fly, still offered a feeble and ineffectual opposition to the advancing troops.

The grey-headed Chobwas of the Shans, in particular, showed a noble example to their men, sword in hand, singly maintaining the unequal contest, nor could signs or gestures of good treatment induce them to forbearance—attacking all who offered to approach them with humane or friendly feelings, they only sought the death which too many of them found. Maha Nemiow himself fell while bravely urging his men to stand their ground, and his faithful attendants being likewise killed by the promiscuous fire while in the act of carrying him off, his body, with his sword, Wonghee's chain, and other insignia of office, were found among the dead. One of the fair Amazons also received a fatal bullet in the breast, but the moment she was seen, and her sex was recognized, the soldiers bore her from the scene of death to a cottage in the rear, where she soon expired.

While this was passing in the interior of the stockades, Sir Archibald Campbell's column, pushing rapidly forward to their rear, met the defeated and panic-struck fugitives in the act of emerging from the jungle, and crossing the Nawine river: the horse-artillery was instantly unlimbered, and opened a heavy fire upon the crowded ford. Another of the Shan ladies was here observed flying on horseback with the defeated remnant of her people; but before she could gain the opposite bank of the river, where a friendly forest promised safety and protection, a shrapnel exploded above her head, and she fell from her horse into the water; but whether killed, or only frightened, could not be ascertained, as she was immediately borne off by her attendants.

This unexpected salute, from a quarter from which no enemy was expected, completed the consternation and defeat of the Burmese left wing; they no longer attempted a junction with their right, or thought of anything beyond immediate safety: seeing our infantry approaching their line of retreat, they quickly dispersed, and betook themselves to the surrounding jungles, where they were protected from pursuit; and at night, assembling in groups, sought the most convenient routes for getting to a distance from the seat of war, and avoiding those who might compel them to rejoin the army.

Few of the Shans were found again in arms; but obliged, in order to escape their Burmese pursuers, to follow a route through insalubrious forests, and unpeopled deserts, numbers whom the sword had spared, perished from famine and disease in the journey to their distant country.

The morning's work was no sooner finished than the troops, piling their arms, were allowed a couple of hours' rest; during which, arrangements were made for returning the same night as far as the ford, where the first division had crossed the Nawine river in the morning; from whence a pathway led towards the enemy's centre, which it was determined to attack at daylight on the following morning, before any certain news of the total defeat of his left could reach the Wongee, and induce him to retire.

The day had long closed ere the rear of the column arrived upon the ground of encampment for the night; where, worn out with fatigue, the troops having finished their hasty meal, sunk down to rest under the canopy of heaven, to recruit their energies and strength for the renewed contest of the morrow. During the night, the events of the day were communicated to the garrison at Prome, and to Sir James Brisbane, who was requested to be in readiness to move forward with the flotilla, as soon as our troops were seen debouching from the jungle in front of Napadee, for the purpose of co-operating in the attack upon that position.

Early on the morning of the 2nd, we were again in motion, following the only track that leads towards the river, through the forest formerly alluded to. The first division led in files along the narrow path, and Brigadier-General Cotton, with the Madras division, which followed in the rear, was directed to explore every opening that presented itself during the march, and to use his utmost endeavours to force a passage through the forest to the right, so as to reach any part of the Burmese position—his coming upon and attacking which, would be the signal for a general assault in front.

After two hours' march, the first division debouching into a plain upon the riverside, opened a communication with the flotilla, and at the same time drew up in front of the stockaded heights of Napadee.

Nothing can exceed the natural obstacles opposed to an advance upon these heights, independent of the artificial means, which the enemy had not failed to employ, to render his situation in every respect secure: the range of hills he occupied, rise in succession along the banks of the Irrawaddy, the second commanding the first, and the third the second; their base is washed by the river on one side, and they are covered, by the forest, from the approach of any force upon the other. The only road to the heights lay along the flat open beach, until checked by the abrupt and rugged termination of the first hill, up the sides of which the troops would have to scramble, exposed to the fire of every gun and musket on its summit; and in addition to these difficulties, the enemy had a numerous body of men stockaded along the wooded bank, which flanks and overlooks the beach for the distance of nearly a mile, in front of the position, and whom it was absolutely necessary to dislodge, before the main body could be attacked. This service was speedily accomplished, by six companies of the Eighty-Seventh regiment penetrating through the jungle in the rear of the flanking works, and carrying one of the stockades which protected the advanced line to the rear; and the enemy, finding himself exposed in this quarter, speedily withdrew his advanced division, leaving the beach open to the bottom of the first hill, round the base of which he still occupied two strong redoubts.

The flotilla now moved forward, and commenced a spirited cannonade on both sides of the river, while the troops were still halted, in the anxious expectation of hearing a fire open from some part of the Madras division to the right. Fruitless and unavailing, however, was every endeavour to penetrate the forest which separated that corps from the Burmese position; and it became at last. necessary to assault it in the front, by the only approach it appeared to have. While the troops were forming for that duty, the brigade of Colonel Elrington, pushing resolutely through the jungle to the rear, succeeded in reaching some of the flanking outworks of the hills, which were attacked so spiritedly by His Majesty's Forty-Seventh and the Thirty-Eighth Native Infantry, as to produce a very favourable diversion to the main attack; the corps destined for which, consisting of His Majesty's Thirteenth, Thirty-Eighth, and Eighty-Seventh regiments, advancing slowly and deliberately, without returning a shot to the continued vollies of their opponents, after possessing themselves of two strong stockades at the bottom of the hill, marched steadily forward, under a heavy fire from the works upon its summit, from which the enemy was finally driven at the point of the bayonet, and so closely followed from hill to hill, that, in the course of an hour, the whole position, nearly three miles in extent, was entirely in our possession.

During the attack, the flotilla pushing rapidly past the works, succeeded in capturing all the boats and stores which had been brought down for the use of the Burmese army.

The defeat of the enemy on the left bank of the Irrawaddy was now complete: between forty and fifty pieces of artillery were captured, and the materiel of his army taken or destroyed: his loss, in killed and wounded, had been very severe; and by desertion alone, he had lost at least a third of his men. The corps of Sudda Woon alone, protected by the intervention of a broad and rapid river, had escaped unpunished, and so carefully were his men concealed from observation, that some time elapsed before it could be ascertained whether his whole force remained in their stockades, or they were only occupied by a rear-guard; it was at length, however, established beyond a doubt, that the right corps still occupied its original ground, and arrangements were immediately made for driving them from it.

On the morning of the 5th, details were embarked for that purpose, on board the flotilla; and a brigade of rockets,

and a mortar-battery, having, during the night, been established on a small island in the middle of the river, within
good range of the stockades, at daybreak, in the morning,
they opened their fire, which was immediately answered
from several pieces of artillery from the opposite shore. The
troops being landed at some distance above the stockades,
commenced the attack in flank and rear, while the batteries and men-of-war's boats cannonaded them in front; and
the enemy, already disheartened, and panic-struck with the
severe punishment they had seen their centre corps sustain,
upon the second, evacuated, after a feeble resistance, their
line upon the river, retreating to a second line of stockades
which they had prepared in the jungle in their rear. Here
they were not allowed a long time to rest: the troops, following up their first success, and unaware of the existence
of any second line, came suddenly upon the crowded works,
whose confused and disorderly defendants, unable to retreat
through the narrow gates of their enclosure, and too much
alarmed to offer effectual opposition, became an easy conquest to the assailants: hundreds fell, in· the desperate effort
to escape, and the nature of the country alone prevented the
whole corps from being taken; which, dispersed and broken,
now fled in all directions through the woods.

Chapter 19

Towards Ava

The road being now clear for an advance upon the capital, the first division with headquarters, and the commissariat of the army, was encamped an the plain of Natalain, eight miles in front of Prome, between the 6th and 8th of December. The second division, under Brigadier-General Cotton, was assembled at some distance to the left, upon a road leading parallel to the river, by: Neoun-ben-zeik to Meaday, by which route he was directed to move in communication with Sir James Brisbane and the flotilla, allowing the first division to precede his march by three days, to give time for its flank movement to take effect upon the strong positions, which the enemy was known to have fortified between Neoun-ben-zeik and Meaday, and in which, it was supposed, he might have concentrated his beaten forces, for the purpose of again endeavouring to check the advance of the British columns. The route of the first division was directed to be by Wattygoon and Seindoup, making a considerable circuit to the eastward, turning all the enemy's river-defences as high as Meaday, in front of which place the whole force was to concentrate.

On the Pegu side, Colonel Pepper of the Madras army, commanding the field corps in that province, was ordered, as previously mentioned, to advance upon Tonghoo, capturing that large city, and threatening the capital on that side. From Arracan we had reason to expect that the force under Brigadier-General Morrison, which had subdued that province, would be able to co-operate with the forces on the Ir-rawaddy, by crossing the mountains and descending into Ava by the pass of Sembeughewn, either forming a junction with Sir Archibald Campbell, or advancing on the capital by the left bank of the river, as circumstances might render most expedient: local difficulties, however, and the unhealthy state of the Arracan army, prevented this movement from taking place; and Colonel Pepper, with his utmost exertions, was un-able to obtain sufficient means of transport, for carrying his orders into effect.

In Assam, the corps of Colonel Richards, after driving the enemy from the province, was prevented from pushing his successes further on that side, by the insalubrious and desert regions, which still separated him from Upper Ava: unpro-vided with adequate stores or means of carriage, his troops, in any attempt to enter the Burmese territories, would have been exposed to the risk of sickness and starvation, with scarcely a prospect of accomplishing any object, even that of a diversion in favour of the main attack. It was therefore left wholly to the army of the Irrawaddy to bring the war to a conclusion; and nothing was wanting in the troops, or forgotten by their leader, which could tend to crown their efforts with success.

The enemy, on their part, had not confided the important interests of the campaign to the valour of one army, or to the natural and artificial strength of one position. The stockades, at Meaday, had been made as strong as the stockading art admitted of, before the Burmese force advanced on Prome, affording a strong point of re-union to the defeated corps, at which they could try their collected strength against an enemy, which had, as yet, only beaten them in detail. At Mel-loone, the reserve under Prince Memiaboo was now esti-mated at fifteen thousand men, and the defences of that place were represented as a *chef-d'oeuvre* of Burmhan fortification. Situated on the west bank of the Irrawaddy, it was separated from our advancing columns by a deep and rapid river, the navigation of which was likewise completely commanded.

The distance from Prome to Ava by land may be estimated at three hundred miles; and although the roads and country upwards are generally more advantageous for military operations than those in the lower provinces, we had still much toil and labour to look forward to, before the army could arrive in the open plains of Upper Ava. Our stock of provisions was calculated for two months' consumption, with the exception of beef for the Europeans, which the country it was supposed would plentifully afford, after we had crossed the districts which had been exhausted and laid waste by the enemy; and arrangements were made for forwarding by water such stores and provisions as from time to time might be required. Our commissariat was conducted by natives, who even volunteered their services as drivers to the foot-artillery, and in more instances than one, showed no reluctance to expose themselves to the fire of their countrymen—testifying great delight at the precision with which the guns, they were attached to, were directed by their new friends and allies.

The officers of the army, no longer subjected to the inconvenience of walking, were now generally mounted on Pegu ponies, and instead of the many miseries and annoyances they had to endure in the march from Rangoon, commenced the second campaign, if not in the style and with the luxuries of Indian warfare, at least in comparative ease and comfort to what they had previously experienced; and both men and officers enjoyed the blessing of robust health, to enable them to bear and overcome any trials or difficulties they might meet with on their journey,

CHAPTER 20

On the March

December 9th. The first division, accompanied by headquarters, began its march; advancing five miles in the direction of Wattygoon, the enclosed nature of the country affording only one spot sufficiently clear for the encampment of the troops. The first mile of our journey passed over a considerable plain of rice-ground; from which the crop had been removed by the enemy while occupying Wattygoon and Simbike—the road bad, and requiring some labour to render it passable for guns—saw neither house, man, nor beast upon the route, and encamped upon what our guides misnamed a plain, overgrown with reeds and elephant grass, six feet in height—wet with the heavy morning dew, the sun, though long after daylight, not yet having reached above the lofty forest, which surrounds this inviting spot.

December 10th. Marched to Wattygoon, and found the stockades, which had formerly been attacked, ten in number, unoccupied by the enemy. The position had been chosen with the usual judgment of the Burmhan engineers, having two sides protected by a deep morass; a jungle covered the approach on the third side—the rear alone was open ground, and the only point from which the works could have been advantageously assailed. The bones of the Sepoys, who were lost in the unsuccessful visit, were lying about the place; it was remarked, however, that few skulls remained, the heads having probably been forwarded to Meaday, as a proof of the valour of the defendants; and the royal order issued on the occasion, proves how much that valour was esteemed.

December 11th. The column marched five miles over a thickly enclosed country, without a house, or any appearance of population. no marks of any part of the Burmese army having followed our present route in their retreat were perceived: it is probable they were too much alarmed and afraid of pursuit, to trust themselves upon any road—their habits and knowledge of the country enabling them to follow jungle tracks, impassable to any but themselves.

December 12th. Marched to Seezengaon, five miles, During the preceding night it rained heavily, and continued to do so, at intervals, during the whole of the day. The road, originally hilly, and of the worst description, was in consequence now rendered nearly impassable, and the artillery and commissariat were unable to complete the short day's journey: broken carts, and dead or exhausted cattle, kept the rear still halted on their original ground; indeed, it not infrequently occurred, traversing these narrow and winding footpaths of the forest, that the front of the line of march reached the new ground of encampment, before the rear could leave the old. Quantities of biscuit and rice were destroyed or damaged by the wet; and the soldiers, pursuing their route through an elephant-grass jungle, fifteen and twenty feet high, were so completely deluged with the water collected in it, as to produce alarming symptoms of disease among them. To complete the misery of our situation, not a spot of open ground could be found to pitch our camp upon: the dry bed of a rivulet presented the only space sufficiently open for erecting our tents, and in this situation, surrounded by a forest of rank and insalubrious reeds, we passed the night. Here cholera broke out among the troops, and ere it could be checked, carried off numerous victims; it was not, however, confined to one division of the force, the Madras division having suffered equally with the first; two British regiments being rendered nearly unfit for service by the ravages of that dreadful disease.

December 14th. On this day the division reached Seindoop, and encamped upon a ridge of woody hills: upon this dry and pleasant ground we halted a day, to enable the commissariat to come up. Our sick list was already much reduced, and the country, abounding in game, partridges, jungle fowls, and deer, afforded amusement and recreation, as well as an agreeable change of scenery to the monotonous, dreary, and unwholesome woodland regions we had lately traversed. Seindoop, formerly a considerable town, had been completely destroyed by fire, and not an inhabitant had yet been met with.

December 16th. Marched to Towkendine, a distance of eleven miles—the road affording frequent testimony of the recent and precipitate retreat of some part of the Burmese army; the ground upon which different parties had bivouacked, was carefully enclosed by strong abbatis, to prevent their being suddenly attacked, if overtaken in their flight. The town of Towkendine stands upon an elevated ridge, with a small river running in its front. The heights had been fortified, and were still occupied by a piquet of the enemy, which retired on the approach of the advance-guard. This post had obviously been prepared to protect the second line of river fortifications from being turned; and its being hastily abandoned was a sufficient proof that the object of the flank movement, of the first division, had been accomplished, by the enemy's retreat upon Meaday.

December 17th. The division marched to the plain of Tabboo, and opened a communication with the flotilla, the enemy having abandoned all their strong posts upon the river up to this point. It only remained to be ascertained. whether or not they still occupied Meaday, and in the course of the forenoon a cavalry patrol was ordered to reconnoitre that place, distant only seven miles. They found the enemy's rearguard in the act of evacuating the last stockade, and following them up, succeeded in taking some prisoners, and four pieces of artillery, which they were about to carry away in a war-boat.

December 18th. Halted, and were joined by the Madras division, the Europeans of which were still suffering severely from the cholera that had attacked them in the jungle during the wet weather.

December 19th. Marched to Meaday, where a scene of misery and death awaited us. Within and around the stockades, the ground was strewed with dead and dying, lying promiscuously together, the victims of wounds, disease, and want. Here and there a small white pagoda marked where a man of rank lay buried; while numerous new-made graves mainly denoted that what we saw was merely the small remnant of mortality which the hurried departure of the enemy had prevented them from burying, The beach and neighbouring jungles were filled with dogs and vultures, whose growling and screaming, added to the pestilential smell of the place, rendered our situation far from pleasant. Here and there a faithful dog might be seen stretched out and moaning over a new-made grave, or watching by the side of his still breathing master; but by far the greater number, deprived of the hand that fed them, went prowling with the vultures among the dead, or lay upon the sand glutted with their foul repast.

As if this scene of death had not sufficed, fresh horrors were added to it by the sanguinary leaders of these unhappy men. Several gibbets were found erected about the stockades, each bearing the mouldering remains of three or four crucified victims, thus cruelly put to death—for perhaps no greater crime than that of wandering from their post in search of food, or, at the very worst, for having followed the example of their chiefs in flying from the enemy.

December 20th. Marched two miles in advance of Meaday, in the vain hope of getting away from the field of death; for fifty miles up the river, and all along the road by which the

162

enemy retired, similar horrors presented themselves; and on some of our grounds of encampment, it was difficult to find room for pitching the tents without previously removing some dead bodies from the spot. Here the Bengal commissariat failed in its supply of beef for the Europeans, and it became necessary to halt that division until cattle could be obtained from the people of the district, who were expected to return to their villages as soon as the enemy's retreat from Meaday was known.

December 21st. Headquarters, with the Madras division, moved towards Melloone, upon which place the Burmese army was now ordered to concentrate. The road, as we advanced, became hilly and extremely bad, requiring the utmost labour and ingenuity of the pioneer corps to enable us to March a daily distance of from six to eight miles. The country through which we passed was wholly depopulated, and the villages either burned or laid in ruins; not a head of cattle, or, indeed, a living thing, except the sick and dying stragglers from the Burmese army, was met with in the march. We appeared to traverse a vast wilderness from which mankind had fled; and our little camp of two thousand men seemed but a speck in the desolate and dreary waste that surrounded it, calling forth, at times; an irksome feeling which could be with difficulty repressed, at the situation of a handful of men in the heart of an extensive empire, pushing boldly forward to the capital, still three hundred miles distant; in defiance of an enemy whose force still outnumbered ours in a tenfold ratio, and without a hope of further reinforcement from our distant ships and depots. An occasional shot from the flotilla, which had got considerably higher up the river, from time to time broke the silence of the desert, and reminded us that we had still much work before us, and were fast approaching to Melloone, where every effort of art and labour had been exhausted to arrest our progress on the imperial city.

December 25th. Marched to Longhee, a pretty, romantically situated town, upon the banks of the Irrawaddy, where a great abundance of game afforded the sportsmen a pleasant break in the tiresome sameness of our journey.

December 26th. The division moved forward ten miles; and, in the course of the day, a flag of truce was sent in from Melloone, with letters communicating the arrival at that place of a commissioner named Kolein Menghie, sent down from Ava, with full powers from the King to conclude a treaty of peace. An answer, expressive of the readiness of the British commissioners to come to terms, being returned, on the following morning, (27th). The division continued its advance, encamping on the banks of the Irrawaddy, about four miles below Melloone, where we were joined by the flotilla, and from whence the enemy's entrenched camp could be observed. We had now marched one hundred and forty miles from Prome, without meeting an inhabitant, along the once thickly-peopled banks of the Irrawaddy; or being able to procure one day's supply from a country formerly abounding in cattle, so effectually had the enemy succeeded in laying waste the line of our advance.

December 28th. The division halted, while two officers visited Melloone, for the purpose of arranging an immediate meeting with the new negotiator. They did not, however, succeed in making any final arrangement, the Burmese chiefs showing strong symptoms of a wish to procrastinate, talking of the expediency of waiting for a propitious time for undertaking a business of such vast importance, and stating that the approaching full moon would prove a favourable period for adjusting matters; upon the whole, the officers appear to have been treated rather cavalierly, and were under the necessity of explicitly declaring, before leaving the place, that as they had failed in the object of their visit, the truce would end with their departure, and the British general would consider himself at liberty to recommence offensive operations as soon as he thought proper.

December 29th. The division again moved forward, and in two hours reached Patanagoh, a town upon the river directly opposite to Melloone. The Irrawaddy at this place is six hundred yards broad, and the fortifications of Melloone, built upon the face of a sloping hill, lay fully exposed to view, within good practice-distance of our artillery. The principal stockade appeared to be a square of about a mile, filled with men, and mounting a considerable number of guns, especially on the water-face; and the whole position, consisting of a succession of stockades, might extend from one to two miles along the beach. In the centre of the great stockade, a handsome new gilt pagoda was observed, which had been raised to the memory of Maba Bandoola, as a testimony of His Majesty's distinguished approbation of the services of that chief, and with a view to incite the present leaders and soldiers of the army, by whom he was much admired, to emulate the noble example he had set them at Donoobew, in preferring death to the loss of his post. On our arrival before the place, the Burmese troops ceased to labour at their defences, and stood in groups gazing at us as we formed upon the opposite shore. Under the stockade, a large fleet lay at anchor, consisting of war-boats, commissariat-boats, accommodation boats, and craft of every description.

We had not long reached our ground, when the loud noise of gongs, drums, and other warlike instruments, attracted our attention to the enemy's works, and crowds of boatmen, with their short oars across their shoulders, were soon seen running to the beach. In an instant, every boat was manned, and in motion up the river. The steam-vessel and flotilla having been detained below the enemy's position, owing to the intricacy of the channel, and until protecting batteries should be formed to keep down the fire of the works along the beach, it became necessary to adopt other measures for preventing the flight of the boats; the artillery was accordingly directed to fire upon them, which speedily checked their further progress, the boatmen either jumping into the river, or returning, with all possible speed, to their former situation.

In the mean time, the flotilla, led by the *Diana* steam-vessel, had got under weigh, when the firing commenced, and was now seen passing close under the enemy's works, without a shot being fired from either side; on reaching the principal stockade, two gilt war-boats, pushing off from the shore, received the *Diana* with every honour, and escorted the squadron until safely anchored at some distance above the place—cutting off all retreat from it by water.

Such unequivocal marks of a desire to prevent further hostility were immediately accepted; the division was forthwith encamped, and during the forenoon a truce was concluded, and arrangements made for entering upon negotiations on the following day.

CHAPTER 21
Talk & Fighting

The Burmese chiefs, at their own request, being permitted to moor a large accommodation-boat in the middle of the river between the two armies, as the place of conference, two o'clock, on the 1st of January, was, fixed for the first meeting with the new delegate from Ava. At the appointed hour, the commissioners of both nations pushed off in boats from their respective sides of the river, and entered the conference vessel nearly at the same moment; the Kee Wongee as joint commissioner, and most of the chiefs we had met at Neoun-ben-zeik, with several others, accompanied His Majesty's deputy, Kolein Menghi.

The countenance of this personage, withered and shrivelled up with age, was strongly expressive of low cunning and dissimulation; at a first glance, he might have passed for a man of seventy, but the vivacity and keenness of a pair of sharp grey eyes, on a nearer view, reduced it ten or fifteen years, and he probably did not much exceed the age of fifty. His person, small and thin, though splendidly dressed up for the occasion, appeared mean and vulgar, contrasted with the easy and dignified demeanour of the Kee Wongee, whose handsome, frank, and open countenance, seemed somewhat abashed and dejected at the remembrance of what had passed at Neoun-ben-zeik, and the present altered and hopeless state of their affairs; but he only said, in answer to our inquiries, that he had suffered much from the dreadful sickness which had carried off so many of his bravest men, and best officers.

After the parties were seated in the boat, Kolein Meng-hi's mouth continued for some time so full of pawn-leaves and betel-nut (to the use of which he seemed to be much addicted) as to prevent him from uttering a word distinctly, while the overflowings of the delicious juice ran in greenish yellow streams down his chin, until checked and absorbed in the long tuft of hair which all Burmese chiefs wear as a mark of distinction on that prominent feature, giving them a most peculiar and goat-like appearance.

When at length he seemed prepared to answer, the business was opened with much solemnity, and the different demands and articles of the treaty—canvassed and discussed by the Burmhan chiefs, of whose style of argument the following may afford a specimen. In answer to the money-demand of one crore of rupees*, Kolein Menghi replied, "In war the expense is not all on one side—we also have expended immense sums, leaving our treasury at the present moment drained and exhausted; it is evident, indeed, that our expenses must have greatly exceeded yours, as we have had to raise and appoint four or five new armies, one after another, and have had at all times since you came to the country, an immense multitude eating the public bread, and receiving the King's money, a great part of whose revenue has been stopped; while you, by means of discipline, and good management, have never required a large force, nor had above a small body of men to pay and provide for."

When told that every English soldier on the opposite bank, cost government nearly two hundred pounds before he reached his present situation, and that every one of the numerous ships which came to Rangoon also cost an immense sum, the Wongee continued, "I also have been a merchant, and engaged in extensive mercantile transactions, but none of my vessels ever cost anything like the sum you mention, but

---

* A million sterling, valuing the rupee at two shillings, the then rate of exchange.

168

whether or not, it is cruel to exact a sum which we cannot pay; our forests contain fine trees, you may cut them down; we could, perhaps, with economy in one year, give you a million baskets of rice; but we do not grow rupees, and have in no way the means of procuring such a sum as you require."

With regard to the cession of Arracan and the restoration of Cassay to its legitimate ruler, Gumbheer Sing, Kolein Menghi again observed, "We are stingy of parting with Arracan, not for its value, but because the honour of the nation is, in some measure, concerned in its retention. The people still look back with-pride and exultation to its conquest, and they would regard its cession as robbing their forefathers, who achieved its subjugation, of their fame and glory. It has been for a long series of years in our possession; its native princes live in comfort and in honour at our capital, and its whole revenue scarcely suffices to discharge the expenses it incurs. Still we would wish to keep the province, and would rather that you asked something in its room.

"With regard to Cassay, it is a barren desert, and of little use to us; our King sent troops into the country, at the request of the proper Rajah, who solicited protection, as a vassal, against a faction that was formed against him: our troops expelled the refractory chiefs from Munnipoore, and the Rajah now resides at Ava: he, and not Gumbheer Sing, is the legitimate Prince of Cassay; he prefers living at our court; but if yon wish his country to be independent, he is the person who should be appointed king."

After four meetings and long discussions on the subject of the terms, in which the Burmese commissioners displayed great meanness, having had recourse to downright begging, when cunning, art, and everything else had failed, the treaty was at length accepted and signed, fifteen days (up to the 18th) being allowed for obtaining the ratification of the King, and the performance of all preliminaries, *viz.* the delivery of all prisoners, and the payment of the first instalment of the money article.

During the interval that ensued, a friendly intercourse was carried on between the two camps, only at times interrupted or disturbed by the enemy's working at, and strengthening his defences, especially during the night, as if aware that nothing. conclusive would result from what had taken place, and that a rupture would ultimately ensue, Strong remonstrances, on this subject, were frequently made to the Burmese chiefs, who, with their usual dexterity and address, parried the accusation of double dealing, attributing to every cause, except the real one, the proceedings we complained of.

Scarcely a day passed without a visit from some chief of rank, to expatiate upon the blessings and happiness that would result from the peace that had been concluded between the two great nations, and stating their expectations that the ratified treaty and prisoners would arrive from Ava long before the period specified.

At length, however, on the 17th, a deputation of three officers of state (two Attawoons and a Woondock) visited the British commissioners, and with much circumlocution gave them to understand, that some unfortunate accident or circumstance, of which they were entirely ignorant, had delayed the arrival of the ratified treaty and prisoners, at the same time declaring that they had not heard from Ava since the treaty was sent up for signature.

The glaring falsehood of this statement at once put the commissioners on their guard against some new attempt of stratagem or treachery, as the chiefs were known to be in daily communication with the capital, boats from which were frequently passing our piquets on the river. They then offered to pay on the spot, a money instalment of four lacs of tickals[*], and give hostages for the performance of the remaining articles of the contract; but, in that case, requested that the British force might return to Prome, to which a most decided negative was given.

---

[*] Tickal, rather more than a rupee.

They next proposed, that, under the same terms, the force should await, on its present ground, the result of their communications to the King; this likewise was positively refused. They at last earnestly entreated that a delay of five or six days might be granted, and were again refused, but told they might communicate to the Prince and the two Wongees, the final and only relaxation from the stipulated agreement that the British commissioners could be induced to grant, *viz.* that if they evacuated Melloone in thirty-six hours, and continued retiring with their forces before the British army upon Ava, hostilities would not be recommenced, and ·the march would be suspended as soon as the ratified treaty should be received.

This proposition being peremptorily rejected, and the armistice having expired, three officers were next day (18th) sent over to Melloone, who formally informed the Wongees, that having again deceived us, and broken their promises and engagements, no further concession could be made, or longer forbearance shown, to a government which was capable of acting such a part; and that after twelve o'clock that night, hostilities would be once more resorted to, and persevered in, until they should amply atone for the perfidy and deception of their; conduct.

At the specified hour of midnight, the British camp was on the alert, and the men engaged with all their life and spirit in throwing up batteries opposite to the selected points of attack in the stockade, which was within good gun-shot range of our bank of the river; the heavy ordnance was also landed from the flotilla during the night, and by ten o'clock next morning twenty-eight pieces of artillery were in battery, and ready to open upon the enemy's defences. Shortly after eleven o'clock the fire commenced from our batteries, and continued without intermission, and with great effect, for nearly two hours, by which time the troops intended for the assault were embarked in boats, under the superintendence of Captain Chads, senior naval officer, at some distance above the place, to ensure their not being carried past it by the force of the stream.

The first Bengal brigade, consisting of His Majesty's Thirteenth and Thirty-Eighth regiments, under Lieutenant-Colonel Sale, was directed to land below the stockade, and attack it by the south-west angle, while three brigades were ordered to land above the place, and after carrying some outworks, to attack it by the northern face. Notwithstanding every previous arrangement, and the utmost exertion of every one employed, the current, together with a strong northerly wind, carried the first brigade, under all the fire of the place, to its destined point of attack, before the other brigades could reach the opposite shore, and being soon formed under the partial cover of a shelving bank, without waiting a moment for the cooperation of the other troops, led by Lieutenant-Colonel Frith, Lieutenant-Colonel Sale (having been wounded in the boats,) moved forward to the assault with a steadiness and regularity that must have struck awe into the minds of their opponents; and in a very short time, entered by escalade, and established themselves in the interior of the works.

A prouder or more gratifying sight has seldom, perhaps, been witnessed, than this mere handful of gallant fellows driving a dense multitude of from ten to fifteen thousand armed men before them, from works of such strength, that even Memiaboo, contrary to all custom, did not think it necessary to leave them until the troops were in the act of carrying them. The other brigades cutting in upon the enemy's retreat, completed their defeat; they were driven, with severe loss, from all their stockades, leaving the whole of their artillery and military stores in our possession. In the house of Prince Memiaboo, cash to the amount of from thirty to forty thousand rupees was found; all his stud was likewise taken.

What was of still more consequence, as affording undeniable proof of the treacherous and perfidious conduct of the Prince, Wongees, and their government, during the late proceedings, both the English and Burmese copies of the treaty were also found in the house, just in the same state as when signed and sealed at the meeting of the 3rd; with every document that passed at Neoun-ben-zeik; and several other papers, written by a priest, styled the Raj Goroo, a spiritual friend and counsellor of the King of Ava, who had been for some time in our lines, and had been employed to carry a pacific message to his Burmhan Majesty.

It is no easy matter to divine what object the court of Ava could have had in view, in opening negotiations they had no intention of abiding by, or what possible result they could have anticipated from a short and profitless delay, which, to us, was in every point of view desirable, as much to allow the men to recover from the debilitating effects of their late sickness, as to afford time for collecting cattle from the interior, and sufficient supplies of every description for prosecuting our journey along a sacked and plundered line of country.

All present at the conference were disposed to think that Kolein Menghi and his colleague were, at the commencement of the negotiations, sincere in their desire of bringing the war to a conclusion; but it is by no means certain that their powers were of so full a nature as they pretended, or that they were authorised to accept of such terms as they agreed to and signed: either they overstepped the limits of their power and commission, or, as is not improbable, the fickle and easily-persuaded King, at the instigation of the crafty priest, who reached Ava at the very time, repented of the measures he had sanctioned, and enjoined his ministers to have recourse once more to duplicity and fraud.

This view of the case was strongly supported by the testimony of those who, about this time, came down from Ava, as well as by other sources of information, representing the King as having been seized by a furious and ungovernable rage, on hearing of our demands, wounding, with a spear, the messenger who brought accounts of what had taken place, and sending down orders to Melloone to: try immediately another battle—a measure strongly advocated by Prince Memiaboo, whose confidence in the strength of his position seems to have been unbounded, and whose headstrong ignorance could neither be governed nor restrained by the dear bought experience of his chiefs.

Memiaboo and his beaten army retired from the scene of their disasters with all possible haste, and the British commander prepared to follow him up without delay; before, however, commencing his march, he despatched a messenger with the un-ratified treaty, to the Kee Wongee, as well to show the Burmese chiefs that their perfidy was discovered, as to give them the means of still performing their engagements; but merely telling the latter, in his note, that in the hurry of departure from Melloone, he had forgotten a document which he might now find more useful and acceptable to his government, than they had a few days previously considered it.

The Wongee and his colleague politely returned their best thanks for the paper, but observed that the same hurry which had caused the loss of the treaty, had compelled them to leave behind a large sum of money, which they also much regretted, and which they were sure the British general only waited an opportunity of returning.

CHAPTER 22

The Final Battle

On the 25th, of January, the army again moved forward, over the most barren and uninteresting country, and by the worst roads that bad yet been met with from Rangoon upwards. On the 3lst,. headquarters were at Zaynan-gheoun, or Earth-oil Creek, near which are extensive petroleum wells; and the whole district, more or less fertile in that useful commodity, is miserable beyond description, in appearance, presenting scarcely a blade of grass or vegetation of any kind, and the cattle, consequently, in a state of starvation. Sanguine hopes had been indulged, that the capture of Melloone would both alarm and humble the violent war faction, which had so long guided the councils of the king of Ava; and these hopes were this day realized, by the arrival, from the capital, of an American missionary, Doctor Price, and Assistant-surgeon Sandford, of the Royal regiment, (who had been taken prisoner some months previous,) on his parole of honour to return again to Ava with his companion; they were also accompanied by four prisoners of war, returned as a compliment from the king.

Such uncouth figures as these poor fellows were, have been seldom exhibited; with their hair uncut, and beards unshorn, since the day they were taken. Mr. Price said, they had been sent for, a few nights previous, between the hours. of eleven and twelve, to the Golden Palace, where they were asked if they would carry a message to the English camp; on stating their readiness to do so, an attawoon, or minister of the interior, made their answer known to the king and council, assembled in another part of the palace, and after some further messages to, and from the council, they were despatched to ascertain the true and real state of affairs between the British and Burmese negotiators; to express the sincere desire. of his Burmhan Majesty for peace; and to bring back a statement of the lowest terms that would he granted to him.

This was immediately furnished, varying little from those offered and accepted at Melloone; and further to evince a corresponding wish for peace, the British general promised, at their request, not to pass Pagahm-mew for twelve days, to afford time for preparing and bringing down the cash from Ava, an acquiescence, however, that had more of courtesy than actual favour in it, as there was little chance of reaching that city, within a couple of days of the period specified. On the following morning, the two delegates departed for Ava, Mr. Price sanguine in his expectations of returning, in a few days, to close the war.

The sources of information now open to us, and the subsequent liberation of all the British and American prisoners at Ava, enabled us to clear up many points in the conduct of the court of Ava, that had, hitherto, been doubtful and obscure. With regard to the perfidy and dissimulation of the Melloone business, it seemed to be the general opinion, that the king, on that occasion, was disposed to be sincere, and would have ratified the treaty, but for the untimely arrival of the false Goroo at Ava, who, it is said, strongly urged the weak monarch against the measure, entreating of him not to accept of such degrading conditions from a mere handful of adventurers, and stating, that the hurry at Melloone arose from our avidity to get possession of the money, after which we would quietly retain all that we had acquired.

Ample evidence was also furnished, that so far from being ignorant of the conduct and aggressions of the Arracan chiefs, which had caused the war, they were fully sanctioned by

His Burmhan Majesty, who, twelve months before hostilities commenced, was devising plans and making arrangements for the conquest of Bengal. Maha Bandoola, then high in favour, was the grand protector of the scheme, and, with a hundred thousand men, which he said His Majesty could with ease assemble, pledged himself for its execution. The king even went the length of consulting a foreign residenter at Ava; and who will longer doubt that war had been resolved on, and success anticipated, when it is stated, on the authority of those who were present on the spot, that Maha Bandoola marched into Arracan, provided with golden fetters, in which the Governor-General of India was to be led captive to Ava?

About this time unpleasant news was received from our small Pegu force, a part of which had been repulsed with heavy loss in an attack upon the strong stockade of Zitoung, the commanding officer, Colonel Conroy, and another officer killed, and several wounded. No time-was, however, lost in remedying this unfortunate failure. Colonel Pepper, commanding in Pegu, immediately advanced upon Zitoung with a stronger detachment, and, after some sharp fighting, routed the enemy with severe loss.

On the 14th of February, the army reached Pakang-yay, having passed Sembeughewn, situated on the opposite shore, and where the road from Arracan reaches the Irrawaddy. At Pakang-yay strong entrenchments had been commenced, but were abandoned by the enemy on the approach of our column. Intimation was also received at this place, that no reinforcement or co-operation was to be expected from Arracan, owing to the sickly state of the troops in that province, and the difficulties attending a movement across the mountains. This information caused no disappointment to the Ava force; things were now fast drawing to a crisis, and it was but natural that those who had had the work should wish to enjoy the reward, undivided with any others. All the people coming down the river, and from the interior, represented the king as being in great alarm, and ready to accede to everything.

On approaching within a few days' march of Pagahm-mew, rumours were again in circulation of a more hostile feeling· on the part of the Court of Ava, which was stated to be making vigorous preparations for a desperate struggle in the neighbourhood of that city; it was, at least, positively known, that on the fall of Melloone, a levy of forty thousand men was ordered, and the people induced to come forward by means of a high bounty, and several honourable privileges and distinctions—every feeling of patriotism and courage being roused by the affecting appeal of a monarch tottering on his throne, and bestowing upon the force which now assembled in his defence; the flattering and animating appellation of Gong-to-doo, or Retrievers of the King's Glory! This army was placed under the command of a savage warrior, styled Nee-Woon-Breen, which has been variously translated, as Prince of Darkness, King of Hell, and Prince of the Setting Sun.

Upon the 8th, when within a day's march from Pagahm-mew all doubts upon the subject of further opposition were at an end, from the certain intelligence, then received, that Nee-Woon-Breen was prepared to meet the advancing force under the walls of that city. On the 9th, the British column moved forward, in order of attack, much reduced by the absence of two brigades, and considerably under two: thousand fighting men; the advance guard was met in the jungle by a strong body of skirmishers; and after maintaining a running fight for several miles, the column, debouching into the open country, discovered the Burmese army, from sixteen to twenty thousand strong, drawn up in an inverted crescent, the wings of which threatened the: little body of assailants on either flank.

Undismayed, however, either by the strength or position of the enemy, the British commander pushed boldly forward for their centre, which was vigorously attacked, the whole weight of his column bearing on that point, and instantly overthrown, leaving the unconnected wings severed from each other, and requiring the utmost activity on their part, to reach a second line of redoubts which had been prepared, for fear of such an event as had taken place, under the walls of Pagahm-mew. The British column, following up the enemy's retreat with the greatest celerity, afforded them little time for rallying in their works, into which they were closely followed by our troops, and again routed with great slaughter: hundreds jumping into the river, to escape their assailants, perished in the water, and, with the exception of two or three thousand men, the whole army dispersed upon the spot. The unfortunate Nee-Woon-Breen himself had no sooner reached Ava than he was most cruelly put to death by order of the king.

On the evening of the 13th, Mr. Price and Mr. Sandford, now liberated, arrived in camp, the former to announce that the king and court of Ava had given in—the last defeat having deprived them of all hope of any good resulting from further opposition, adding that our terms had been accepted and agreed to, but neither returning the prisoners nor bringing the first instalment of the money-payment (twenty-five lacs of rupees) as directed; explaining, however, that everything demanded was in readiness to be delivered, but that the king demurred about letting the cash out of his hands, from an idea that, after its payment, we would still keep his country, as under similar circumstances he would himself most assuredly do. He was, therefore, anxious to know if we could not be prevailed upon to accept of six lacs upon the spot, receiving the other nineteen on the arrival of the army at Prome, begging, at the same time, that in any case the force should not approach nearer to the capital, a positive refusal was given to every part of the request; and on the following morning, Mr. Price returned to Ava, stating the certainty of his coming back in a day or two, accompanied by some of the Burmhan ministers, for the purpose of making a final settlement.

The country from Pagahm-mew to Ava is most beautiful, extensive plains of the finest land watered by the Irrawaddy, interspersed with evergreen woods only sufficiently large to give beauty and variety to the scenery; and the banks of the river so thickly studded with villages, pagodas, temples, monasteries, and other handsome buildings, as to give,: under one *coup-d'oeil*, all the charms of a richly varied landscape, with the more sterling beauties of a populous and fertile country.

The army, continuing to advance, was met at Yandaboo, only forty-five miles from Ava, by Mr. Price, and two ministers of state, accompanied by the prisoners* and the stipulated sum of twenty-five lacs of rupees; empowered to state without reserve, that they had given in, and bearing an authority under the sign manual, to accept of, and sign, such terms as we might insist upon. On the 24th of February, the treaty was, for the second time, settled, and finally signed; the Burmese government, at the same time, engaging to furnish boats for the conveyance of a great part of the force to Rangoon.

* * * * * *

Here the war may be considered at an end: a war into which the government of India had been forced, and of a more serious and protracted nature than any in which our Eastern empire had been engaged for a long series of years; distinguished from all others, by the obdurate and determined perseverance of the enemy, and characterized by a series of difficulties, obstacles, and privations to which few armies have been for so long a period subjected.

One latent feeling of disappointment alone remained; men and officers felt proud in having at last compelled our stubborn foe to sign a peace honourable and advantageous to India, as it was humiliating and inglorious to the court of Ava; proud that the utmost wishes of our government had been realized, and the service we were employed on, to the fullest extent; completed. Still we were only three marches from the capital of the despot, the source from which the war and all its

---

*Mr. Judson (an American missionary) and his wife, Mr. Gouger, a British merchant, and several others who had been taken during the ·war.

lengthened misery had sprung, and from the primary cause of so much suffering and bloodshed, and it was not in the nature of a British soldier to turn his back on the Golden City, the supposed riches of which we had hoped to share, without some feelings of regret.

The conquest of the capital of Alompra, it was urged by some, who took a more general view of the case, would have had a good effect upon the whole Eastern world; and its reduction would, no doubt, have been desirable, could all the advantages of the peace concluded at Yandaboo have been guaranteed on our arrival there; but those best acquainted with the strange people we had to deal with, are well aware, that every sacrifice they were disposed to make, was to ensure the preservation of the city; that once subdued, the court would have; fled for a season, to some distant part of their extensive empire, and have left the Indian government the mere honour of having conquered a country which they could not retain; and from which necessity would soon compel them to retire without gain or profit, and with the ruinous burthen of the expenses of the war, wholly upon their own shoulders, instead of the many advantages that must attend the acceptance of their terms.

Nor could it even be urged that celerity of movement might enable us to reach the capital before the court had left it: the very idea of attempting to cope in that point with men who can change their places of abode with the facility of Bedoueen Arabs was preposterous.

That Ava would have fallen, no man will doubt; taken most assuredly it would have been, had the attempt been made; and perhaps a handsome booty might have enriched the captors; but his could only have been attempted at a great political risk, and the probable sacrifice of every object for which the government of India had been so long contending; for we should undoubtedly have found neither King nor Ministers to treat with; and with all the honour and glory of subduing the capital, we should most probably have occupied merely the deserted space within its walls.

CHAPTER 23

Concluding Remarks

The government, customs, and manners of the Burmese have been so well described in the interesting journal of Captain Symes, who· had an excellent opportunity of viewing them in a time of profound peace, that it would amount almost to presumption in anyone, to enter upon that subject, whose acquaintance with the nation, and knowledge of the character of the people, were drawn from observations made during a time of war; when their habits and deportment were liable to constant change, according to the variety of novel circumstances in which they were placed, and with their government, during the whole of that period, in a most distracted and unsettled state. A few remarks, however, upon the trade and productions of the country, drawn from authentic sources, may not prove unacceptable.

It does not exceed six years since European goods were first introduced, in any quantity, into Pegu and Ava; and since that period the demand for them has annually increased threefold, and would continue to do so in a much greater ratio, as the knowledge of the traders, with the taste and wants of the people, became more perfect.

There is no country in the east so well situated for an inlet to our trade; and under a better form of government, a ready market would be found for a large consumption of British merchandise, as there is scarcely an article of dress among the natives, that is not already British, or certain to become so.

Rangoon has long been a mart to the Siamese, where they annually bartered the produce of their country, such as raw silk, sticklac, &c., with the merchants settled at that place; but owing to the rapacious character of the Burmese authorities, it has never been carried to the extent, which the wants and disposition of the people would, under other circumstances, most certainly have led to.

But for the grievous exactions and oppressive impositions of the government of Ava, and its numerous functionaries, the Chinese would, long since, have opened an extensive trade with the British settlers at Rangoon; and a safe market for· their goods alone is wanting, to ensure a large proportion of the Canton trade being carried on over land through Ava; opening at once a wide and important inlet to the commerce of Great Britain. Even before the war, notwithstanding existing abuses, and the insecurity attending mercantile transactions throughout the kingdom, silk, tea, vermilion, gold, and silver, were imported in considerable quantities from China into Ava; and, with confidence once established in the government, the general produce of the empire would pour in to any extent that might be required.

The trade of Pegu is still in its infancy, and its productions and resources wholly neglected by its present rulers. Lead, tin, and iron, of a fine quality, are found an the Siamese frontier of Tenassarim, and all along that range of country, nearly as far north as Ava: sticklac is procurable in large quantities; kutch, bees-wax, and elephants-teeth in great abundance; and cotton, if encouraged, might be had to a large extent.

The climate and soil of Pegu are peculiarly favourable to the growth of indigo, which may be cultivated of as fine a quality as any grown in Bengal, and without the crops being subject to the same risk of failure: but in teak-timber, especially, Pegu surpasses all other countries for the cheapness, variety and quantity of that valuable article.

The forests of Sarrawaddy, and the other woodland districts of Pegu, contain an inexhaustible supply of the finest timber. Crooked teak timber, for first rate men of war, may be bought at Rangoon, at a cheapness of rate greatly below what it can be purchased for on the Malabar coast, or probably in any other part of the world—the numerous creeks and rivers that intersect the country enabling the Burmese government to bring it from the woods to the market at a very trifling expense.

The whole of these extensive forests either appertain unto the crown, or are held at the will of the sovereign by the princes of the blood, or the high nobles, whose services, situation or estimation at the court, entitle them to a grant of land. During the dry season, the timber is cut down-and rafted by the woodmen; or royal slaves, as they are termed: and in the rains, when the river rises, and its various branches fill, is conducted by numerous streams into the Irrawaddy, and floated down river to Rangoon, or Bassein, for sale.

The port of Rangoon is admirably adapted for shipbuilding. The river rises in spring tides, from twenty-five to twenty-eight feet; the natives are strong and robust, and, with a little practice, would become expert workmen. When the British army took possession of the place, they found a twenty-eight gun frigate on the stocks for the Imaum of Muscat; it has since been launched, and is considered by judges, both as to model and workmanship, a very fine vessel: she was built wholly by Burmese workmen, under the direction of an English shipbuilder, and most probably, at one-third less expense than it would have cost in any other dockyard in the world.

Pegu is extremely fertile in rice, and its coasts most productive in salt: in these indispensable articles of Burmhan food, Ava is, in a great measure, dependent on its southern provinces. Large quantities of rice, salt-fish, and salt, are annually sent up the Irrawaddy, for the consumption of the capital, and the sterile districts to its northward; and, in whatever way the two countries may have managed in the times of their mutual independence, it is certain, that Ava could not, at the present day, or, at all events for some years, exist without assistance from Pegu. It is true, that the cultivation of the land in Upper Ava may have been neglected; the warlike habits of the people, and insatiable love of conquest in their rulers, leaving the Carians and cultivators, in the fertile deltas of Pegu, to supply the nation with grain, while the men of the less favoured districts were either engaged in, or obliged to be in constant readiness and training, for some new invasion of their ambitious monarch. These unsettled habits among the people have rendered them averse to work; and while their few wants are supplied, and rice and fish selling moderately in the bazaar neither they, nor their rulers, seem to care from whence they come.

To the northward of Ava, there are mines of gold, silver, and precious stones—rubies and sapphires of the finest description—but as all mines, throughout the kingdom, form one of the numerous royal monopolies, and are only worked at particular times, by special order from the sovereign, one of whose titles is "proprietor of the mines of rubies, gold, and silver," the nation derives little benefit from their existence. No specie, however plentiful it may be, is permitted to be exported, and this formed one great drawback to the trade with Ava; the merchants, unable to carry off all their profits or returns in produce, were often under the necessity of suspending their sales, even when the demand was greatest, and the native merchants, ready to pay for their goods in silver or gold, or to smuggle the money into vessels at a great risk of seizure and consequent: forfeiture.

Vast sums are annually expended by the monarch and his court, in building and gilding pagodas, in the middle of which images of Ghaudma, made of solid gold, are frequently buried, particularly in the splendid and very sacred buildings of this description in the neighbourhood of the capital.

It is to be hoped, that many of the mercantile advantages, above alluded to, will still accrue to this country, from the retention of the ceded provinces of Tenasserim.

The new settlement of Amherst town, in particular, is well

situated as a mart for the Siamese, Burmese, and even for the Chinese. Its situation is on the east bank of the Saluoen river, which empties itself into the gulf of Martaban, and now forms the boundary between the province of Yeh, and the Burmese province of Martaban. The whole of these provinces, now thinly peopled, will soon be abundantly populous: the inhabitants of Pegu, and even Ava, already well acquainted with the difference between their own arbitrary laws and our more liberal and enlightened code of jurisprudence, will fly from the oppressive measures of their own chiefs, and flock to the ceded districts, to enjoy the privileges of a milder sway; and where security of property, and encouragement to industry, will soon convert these long ill-governed provinces into one of the finest countries in the east.

The climate is most excellent—greatly surpassing that of Bengal, Madras, or perhaps any other spot situated in so high a latitude. During the sickness at Rangoon, when the European convalescents required a change of air, they were sent round in great numbers to Mergui, where they rapidly recovered, and were soon enabled to rejoin their corps in perfect health. The harbour of Mergui is good, and contains safe anchorage for vessels of considerable burthen.

It may still be asked, as a question of no small interest and importance, whether the signal defeats, exemplary punishment, and recent losses, experienced by the court of Ava, will effectually deter that restless and vindictive government from offering future molestation to the Company's territories, and from again disturbing the peace and tranquillity of the eastern world; and a very short review of their present situation, and of the state of public feeling in the country, may probably suffice to place the matter beyond a doubt.

No nation ever commenced hostilities so thoroughly ignorant of the power and resources of their adversaries, and so grossly deceived as to their own strength and means, as was the court of Ava in the late rupture with British India; and no nation ever required so many convincing proofs of their error and mistake, as were afforded during the contest that ensued. Not satisfied with the signal defeat of every force they brought into the field; and undismayed by the steady and unchecked advance of the British army upon their capital, the king and his advisers stubbornly refused to yield, and continued their preparations for obstinate, though fruitless, opposition, long after more than half the kingdom had quietly submitted.

Insensible to the convulsed and almost revolted state of the country, to the dispirited and subdued valour of his troops, the despot seemed resolved to meet the approaching crisis, and rather to risk the loss of his crown in the national convulsion which his obstinacy might produce, than to accept of any terms from the invaders of his kingdom. Mild and lenient as were the proffered conditions, viewed as coming from a victorious enemy, who had been forced by insult and aggression into a war, carried on for two years at a vast expense in blood and treasure, and addressed to the aggressor, already trembling on his throne, infatuation can alone account for his refusing to subscribe to such demands; leading us to consider the prospect of a termination to the contest hopeless, from anything short of the extinction of the reigning family.

The peculiar distrust and jealousy which have long been recognised as leading traits in the character of the Burmese government, must account for the singular blindness and obstinacy of their conduct on this occasion. A Burmese monarch has never been known to make war for any other object than that of conquest, and the aggrandisement of his kingdom; and no instance is on record of one of the race having relinquished a single acre of what he could retain. Judging, then, from his own system and constant practices, he might naturally enough conclude, that such also would be our policy; and it must, at all events, have been far beyond a Burmese king's belief, to credit an offer of voluntarily giving up so fine a territory upon his acquiescence in such terms as were to be imposed.

Surrounded, too, by flatterers, who found it profitable to themselves to keep alive his fears, and buoy up his false hopes and expectations, the deluded Monarch was induced to turn a deaf ear to every overture that was made; and, in the last extremity, was undoubtedly prepared for flight into the woods, under an impression that his only chance of safety consisted in an active perseverance in hostility, which his advisers persuaded him would render the retention of his country troublesome, and profitless, and that ultimately we should be glad to get rid of our acquisitions upon any terms. Such was, until the very last stage of hostile operations, the ruling policy of the cabinet of Ava—a policy that required the greatest nicety of management to overcome. Negotiation alone would never have gained either concession or any guarantee against future annoyances; but when backed by severe and exemplary punishment, and steadiness in the prosecution of our just demands—by the invincible character of the army, and its dictating attitude at the gates of the capital, the King could no longer refuse to listen to the moderate and temperate appeal of an enemy so situated.

Persuaded, at length, that he might still retain his kingdom, and place unqualified reliance in our promises, he, with barbarous tokens of sincerity, paved the way for peace, by the disgrace or death of his principal war advisers, and humbly accepted of every condition the British Commissioners thought proper to dictate.

The cession of Arracan amply provides for the freedom from Burmese interference with our Indian territories on that side: our troublesome neighbours are now confined within their ancient boundaries by the lofty Anoupectoumiew; and the King is not ignorant that, should he again offend, we can march a force across these mountains, and appear on the Irrawaddy, from our post at Aing, in eight or ten days, and probably· reach his capital within a month. Besides, he is aware that the feeling and character of his subjects have undergone a total change: for, without asserting that they either respect or love us, we may at least insist that they assuredly fears us; and whatever may have been, or still may be, their opinion of themselves, they are well satisfied, from sad experience, that they would have little chance with such a force as the Indian government can send into the field.

The King of Ava, under such circumstances, can have neither interest nor motive in troubling us again. That he may intrigue and endeavour to deceive is probable, and consistent with, the faithless character of his government. That he may still use a high, and even insolent tone, pretend to treat us slightingly, and continue to style himself "Lord of Earth and Air," is to be expected; but many years will probably pass before we hear of another hostile threat from that quarter. Let him then vaunt and boast, and let us smile at his harmless vanity and arrogant imbecility.

LEONAUR

ALSO FROM LEONAUR

AVAILABLE IN SOFTCOVER OR HARDCOVER WITH DUST JACKET

SEPOYS, SIEGE & STORM *by Charles John Griffiths*—The Experiences of a young officer of H.M.'s 61st Regiment at Ferozepore, Delhi ridge and at the fall of Delhi during the Indian mutiny 1857.

CAMPAIGNING IN ZULULAND *by W. E. Montague*—Experiences on campaign during the Zulu war of 1879 with the 94th Regiment.

THE STORY OF THE GUIDES *by G. J. Younghusband*—The Exploits of the Soldiers of the famous Indian Army Regiment from the northwest frontier 1847 - 1900..

ZULU: 1879 *by D.C.F. Moodie & the Leonaur Editors*—The Anglo-Zulu War of 1879 from contemporary sources: First Hand Accounts, Interviews, Dispatches, Official Documents & Newspaper Reports.

THE RECOLLECTIONS OF SKINNER OF SKINNER'S HORSE *by James Skinner*—James Skinner and his 'Yellow Boys' Irregular cavalry in the wars of India between the British, Mahratta, Rajput, Mogul, Sikh & Pindarree Forces.

TOMMY ATKINS' WAR STORIES 14 FIRST HAND ACCOUNTS—Fourteen first hand accounts from the ranks of the British Army during Queen Victoria's Empire Original & True Battle Stories Recollections of the Indian Mutiny With the 49th in the Crimea With the Guards in Egypt The Charge of the Six Hundred With Wolseley in Ashanti Alma, Inkermann and Magdala With the Gunners at Tel-el-Kebir Russian Guns and Indian Rebels Rough Work in the Crimea In the Maori Rising Facing the Zulus From Sebastopol to Lucknow Sent to Save Gordon On the March to Chitral Tommy by Rudyard Kipling

CHASSEUR OF 1914 *by Marcel Dupont*—Experiences of the twilight of the French Light Cavalry by a young officer during the early battles of the great war in Europe.

TROOP HORSE & TRENCH *by R. A. Lloyd*—The experiences of a British Lifeguardsman of the household cavalry fighting on the western front during the First World War 1914-18.

THE EAST AFRICAN MOUNTED RIFLES *by C. J. Wilson*—Experiences of the campaign in the East African bush during the First World War.

THE FIGHTING CAMELIERS *by Frank Reid*—The exploits of the Imperial Camel Corps in the desert and Palestine campaigns of the First World War.

Printed in the United Kingdom
by Lightning Source UK Ltd.
122886UK00001B/51/A